COMPUTER SCIENCE, TECHNOLOGY AND APPLICATIONS

DATA MINING

PRINCIPLES, APPLICATIONS AND EMERGING CHALLENGES

COMPUTER SCIENCE, TECHNOLOGY AND APPLICATIONS

COMPUTER SCIENCE, TECHNOLOGY AND APPLICATIONS

DATA MINING

PRINCIPLES, APPLICATIONS AND EMERGING CHALLENGES

HAROLD L. CAPRI
EDITOR

nova publishers
New York

Library of Congress Cataloging-in-Publication Data

Data mining (Nova Science Publishers)
Data mining : principles, applications and emerging challenges / [edited by] Harold L. Capri.
pages cm. -- (Computer science, technology and applications)
Includes bibliographical references and index.
ISBN 978-1-63463-738-1 (softcover)
1. Data mining. I. Capri, Harold L., editor. II. Ma, Xiaolei, 1985- Transit passenger origin inference using smart card data and GPS data. III. Title.
QA76.9.D343D365 2014
006.3'12--dc23
2014047181

Published by Nova Science Publishers, Inc. † New York

CONTENTS

PREFACE

Data mining is an area of research where appropriate methodological research and technical means are experienced to produce useful knowledge from different types of data. Data mining techniques use a broad family of computationally intensive methods that include decision trees, neural networks, rule induction, machine learning and graphic visualization. This book discusses the principles, applications and emerging challenges of data mining.

Chapter 1 - To improve customer satisfaction and reduce operation costs, transit authorities have been striving to monitor their transit service quality and identify the key factors to attract the transit riders. Traditional manual data collection methods are unable to satisfy the transit system optimization and performance measurement requirement due to their expensive and labor-intensive nature. The recent advent of passive data collection techniques (e.g., Automated Fare Collection and Automated Vehicle Location) has shifted a data-poor environment to a data-rich environment, and offered the opportunities for transit agencies to conduct comprehensive transit system performance measures. Although it is possible to collect highly valuable information from ubiquitous transit data, data usability and accessibility are still difficult. Most Automatic Fare Collection (AFC) systems are not designed for transit performance monitoring, and additional passenger trip information cannot be directly retrieved. Interoperating and mining heterogeneous datasets would enhance both the depth and breadth of transit-related studies. This study proposed a series of data mining algorithms to extract individual transit rider's origin using transit smart card and GPS data. The primary data source of this study comes from the AFC system in Beijing, where a passenger's boarding stop (origin) and alighting stop (destination) on a flat-rate bus are not recorded on the check-in and check-out scan. The bus arrival time at each stop can be inferred from GPS data, and individual passenger's boarding stop is then estimated by fusing the identified bus arrival time with smart card data. In addition, a Markov chain based Bayesian decision tree algorithm is proposed to mine the passengers' origin information when GPS data are absent. Both passenger origin mining algorithms are validated based on either on-board transit survey data or personal GPS logger data. The results demonstrate the effectiveness and efficiency of the proposed algorithms on extracting passenger origin information. The estimated passenger origin data are highly valuable for transit system planning and route optimization.

Chapter 2 - Differentiation between learners, adapted and personalized learning are interesting research directions on technology for human learning today. This issue leads to the design of educational systems integrating strategies for learners' monitoring to assist each by evaluating his knowledge and skills in one hand and detecting and analyzing his errors and obstacles in the other hand. In this respect, formative evaluation is the process used to capture data on the strengths and weaknesses of a learner. These data, to be useful, must be objectively analyzed so that it can be used to manage the following sessions. There are different data mining tools using different algorithms for data analysis and knowledge extraction. Can we use these tools in computer based systems? In such cases, is it possible to directly use a variety of general-purpose algorithms for learning data analysis? The authors discuss in this paper a learning cycle that can be a learning session with feedback loop integrating formative evaluation followed by knowledge extraction process using data mining algorithms. The author's experiments, presented in this work, shows a set of tests, about the exploration of learners' errors, obtained from a self e-learning by doing tool for the algorithmic domain. The authors used the data mining algorithms implemented in the Weka tool: the C4.5 algorithm for classification, A Priori one for association rules deduction and K-Means for clustering. The results given by these experiments have proved the interest of classification and clustering as implemented in Weka. However, the A priori algorithm gives in some cases results difficult to interpret so that it needs a specific optimization to get adequate frequents detection.

Chapter 3 - Since the concept of 'failed states' was coined in the early 1990s, it has come to occupy a top tier position in the international peace and security's agenda. This study uses data mining techniques to examine the effect of various social, economic and political factors on states' failure at the global level. Data mining techniques use a broad family of computationally intensive methods that include decision trees, neural networks, rule induction, machine learning and graphic visualization. Three artificial neural network models: multi-layer perceptron neural network (MLP), radial basis function neural network (RBFNN) and self-organizing maps neural network (SOM) and one machine learning technique (support vector machines [SVM]) are compared to a standard statistical method (linear discriminant analysis (LDA). The variable sets considered are demographic pressures, movement of refugees, group paranoia, human flight, regional economic development, economic decline, de-legitimization of the state, public services' performance, human rights status, security apparatus, elites' behavior and the role played by other states or external political actors. The study shows how it is possible to identify various dimensions of states' failure by uncovering complex patterns in the dataset, and also shows the classification abilities of data mining techniques.

Chapter 4 - This paper presents a novel self-adaptive grammar-guided genetic programming proposal for mining association rules. It generates individuals through a context-free grammar, which allows of defining rules in an expressive and flexible way over different domains. Each rule is represented as a derivation tree that shows a solution (described using the language) denoted by the grammar. Unlike existing evolutionary algorithms for mining association rules, the proposed algorithm only requires a small number of parameters, providing the possibility of discovering association rules in an easy way for non-expert users. More specifically, this algorithm does not require any threshold, and uses a novel parent selector based on a niche-crowding model to group rules. This approach keeps the best individuals in a pool and restricts the extraction of similar rules by analysing the instances covered. The author's compare our approach with the G3PARM algorithm, the first grammar-guided genetic programming algorithm for the extraction of association rules. G3PARM was described as a high-performance algorithm, obtaining important results and overcoming the drawbacks of current exhaustive search and evolutionary algorithms. Experimental results show that the author's new proposal obtains very interesting and reliable rules with higher support values.

In: Data Mining
Editor: Harold L. Capri
ISBN: 978-1-63463-738-1

Chapter 1

TRANSIT PASSENGER ORIGIN INFERENCE USING SMART CARD DATA AND GPS DATA

Xiaolei Ma*[*1], Ph.D. and Yinhai Wang[2], Ph.D.
[1]School of Transportation Science and Engineering,
Beihang University, Beijing, China
[2]Department of Civil and Environmental Engineering,
University of Washington, Seattle, WA, US

ABSTRACT

To improve customer satisfaction and reduce operation costs, transit authorities have been striving to monitor their transit service quality and identify the key factors to attract the transit riders. Traditional manual data collection methods are unable to satisfy the transit system optimization and performance measurement requirement due to their expensive and labor-intensive nature. The recent advent of passive data collection techniques (e.g., Automated Fare Collection and Automated Vehicle Location) has shifted a data-poor environment to a data-rich environment, and offered the opportunities for transit agencies to conduct comprehensive transit system performance measures. Although it is possible to collect highly valuable information from ubiquitous transit data, data usability and accessibility are still difficult. Most Automatic Fare Collection (AFC) systems are not designed for transit performance monitoring, and additional passenger trip information cannot be directly

[*] Email: xiaolm@uw.edu

retrieved. Interoperating and mining heterogeneous datasets would enhance both the depth and breadth of transit-related studies. This study proposed a series of data mining algorithms to extract individual transit rider's origin using transit smart card and GPS data. The primary data source of this study comes from the AFC system in Beijing, where a passenger's boarding stop (origin) and alighting stop (destination) on a flat-rate bus are not recorded on the check-in and check-out scan. The bus arrival time at each stop can be inferred from GPS data, and individual passenger's boarding stop is then estimated by fusing the identified bus arrival time with smart card data. In addition, a Markov chain based Bayesian decision tree algorithm is proposed to mine the passengers' origin information when GPS data are absent. Both passenger origin mining algorithms are validated based on either on-board transit survey data or personal GPS logger data. The results demonstrates the effectiveness and efficiency of the proposed algorithms on extracting passenger origin information. The estimated passenger origin data are highly valuable for transit system planning and route optimization.

Keywords: Automated fare collection system, transit GPS, passenger origin inference, Bayesian decision tree, Markov chain

INTRODUCTION

According to the Census of 2000 in the United States, approximately 76% people chose privately owned vehicles to commute to work in 2000 (ICF consulting, 2003). Recent studies conducted by the 2009 American Community Survey indicate 79.5% of home-based workers drive alone for commuting (McKenzie and Rapino, 2009). Many developing countries, e.g., China, also rely on privately owned vehicles to commute. For example, more than 34% of the Beijing residents chose cars as their primary travel mode while only 28.2% chose transit in 2010 (Beijing Transportation Research Center, 2012). Public transit has been considered as an effective countermeasure to reduce congestion, air pollution, and energy consumption (Federal Highway Administration, 2002). According to 2005 urban mobility report conducted by Texas Transportation Institute (2005), travel delay in 2003 would increase by 27 percent without public transit, especially in those most congested metropolitan cites of U.S., public transit services have saved more than 1.1 billion hours of travel time. Moreover, public transit can help enhance business, reduce city sprawl through the transit oriented development (TDO). During certain emergency scenarios, public transit can even act as a safe and efficient transportation mode for evacuation (Federal Highway Administration, 2002). Based on the aforementioned reasons, it is of critical importance to improve the efficiency of public transit system, and promote more roadway users to utilize public transit. To fulfill these objectives, transit agencies need to understand the areas where improvements can be further made, and whether community goals are being met, etc. A well-developed performance measure system will facilitate decision making for transit agencies. Transit agencies can evaluate the transit ridership trends with fare policy changes and identify where and when better transit service should be provided. In addition, transit agencies are also required to summarize transit performance statistics for reporting to either the National Transit Database (Kittelson & Associates et al., 2003), or the general public who are interested knowing how well transit service is being provided. Nevertheless, developing a set of structured performance measures often requires a large amount of data and the corresponding domain knowledge to process and analyze these data. These obstacles create challenges for transit agencies to spend time and effort undertaking. Traditionally, transit agencies heavily rely on manual data collection methods to gather transit operation and planning data (Ma et al., 2012). However, traditional data collection methods (e.g., travel diary, survey, etc.) are fairly costly and difficult to implement at a multiday level due to their low response rate and accuracy. Transit agencies have spent tremendous manpower and resource undertaking manual data collections, and consumed a significant amount of energy and time to post-process the raw data. With advances in information technologies in intelligent transportation systems (ITS), the availability of public transit data has been increasing in the past decades, which has gradually shifted public transit system into a data-rich paradigm. Automatic Fare Collection (AFC) system and Automatic Vehicle Track (AVL) system are two common passive data collection methods. AFC system, also known as Smart Card system, records and processes the fare related information using either contactless or contact card to complete the financial transaction (Chu, 2010). There exist two typical types of AFC systems: entry-only AFC system and distance-based AFC system. In the entry-only AFC system, passengers are only required to swipe their smart cards over the card reader during boarding, while passengers need to check in and check out during both their boarding and alighting procedures for the distance-based AFC system. AVL and AFC technologies hold substantial promise for transit performance analysis and management at a relative low cost. However, historically, both AVL and AFC data have not been used to their full potentials. Many AVL and AFC systems do not archive data in a readily utilized manner (Furth, 2006). AFC system is initially designed to reduce workloads of tedious manual fare collections, not for transit operation and planning purposes, and thereby, certain critical information, such as specific spatial location for each transaction, may not be directly captured. AVL system tracks transit vehicles' geospatial locations by Global Positioning System (GPS) at either a constant or varying time interval. The accuracy of GPS occasionally suffers from signal loss due to tall building obstructions in the urban area (Ma et al., 2011). Both of the AFC system and AVL system have their inherent drawbacks in monitoring transit system performance, and require analytical approaches to eliminate the erroneous data, remedy the missing values, and mine the unseen and indirect information.

The remainder of this paper is organized as follows: transit smart card data and GPS data are described in the section 2. Based on these data sets, a data fusion method is initially proposed to integrate with roadway geospatial data to estimate transit vehicles arrival information. And then, a Bayesian decision tree algorithm is presented to estimate each passenger's boarding stop when GPS data are unavailable. Considering the expensive computational burden of decision tree algorithms, Markov-chain property is taken into account to reduce the algorithm complexity. On-board survey and GPS data from the Beijing transit system are used to test and verify the proposed algorithms. Conclusion and future research efforts are summarized at the end of this paper.

RESEARCH BACKGROUND

Data from AFC system and AVL system are the two primary sources in this study. Beijing Transit Incorporated began to issue smart cards in May 10, 2006. The smart card can be used in both the Beijing bus and subway systems. Due to discounted fares (up to 60% off) provided by the smart card, more than 90% of the transit riders pay for their transit trips with their smart cards in 2010 (Beijing Transportation Research Center, 2010). Two types of AFC systems exist in Beijing transit: flat fare and distance-based fare. Transit riders pay at a fixed rate for those flat fare buses when entering by tapping their smart cards on the card reader. Thus, only check-in scans are necessary. For the distance-based AFC system, transit riders need to swipe their smart cards during both check-in and check-out processes. Transit riders need to hold their smart cards near the card reader device to complete transactions when entering or exiting buses. Smart card can be used in Beijing subway system as well, where passengers need to tap their smart card on top of fare gates during entering and existing subway stations. Both boarding and alighting information (time and location) are recorded by the fare gates. Although transit smart card exhibits its superiority on its convenience and efficiency, there are still the following issues to prevent transit agencies fully taking advantages of smart card for operational purposes:

- Passenger boarding and alighting information missing

Due to a design deficiency in the smart card scan system, the AFC system on flat fare buses does not save any boarding location information, whereas the AFC system stores boarding and alighting location, except for boarding time information on distance-based fare buses. Key information stored in the database includes smart card ID, route number, driver ID, transaction time, remaining balance, transaction amount, boarding stop (only available for distance-based fare buses), and alighting stop (only available for distance-based fare buses).

- Massive data sets

More than 16 million smart card transactions data are generated per day. Among these transactions, 52% are from flat-rate bus riders. These smart card transactions are scattered in a large-scale transit network with 52386 links and 43432 nodes as presented in figure 1:

Figure 1. Beijing Transit GIS Network.

- Limited external data with poor quality

Only approximate 50% of transit vehicles in Beijing are equipped with GPS devices for tracking. GPS data are periodically sent to the central server at a pre-determined interval of 30 seconds. However, the collected GPS data suffer from two major data quality issues: (1) vehicle direction information is missing; (2) GPS points fluctuation (Lou, et al., 2009). Map matching algorithms are needed to align the inaccurate GPS spatial records onto the road network. In addition, most of transit routes are not designed to have fixed schedules because of high ridership demands, and only certain routes with a long distance or headway follow schedules at each stop (Chen, 2009). The above characteristics of the Beijing AFC and AVL systems create more challenges to process and mine useful information.

It is noteworthy that the AFC system used in Beijing is not a unique case. Most cities in China also employ the similar AFC system where passengers' origin information is absent, such as Chongqing City (Gao and Wu, 2011), Nanning City (Chen, 2009), Kunming City (Zhou et al., 2007). In other developing countries, such as Brazil, AFC system does not record any boarding location information as well (Farzin, 2008). Therefore, a solution for passenger boarding and alighting information extraction is beneficial to those transit agencies with imperfect SC data internationally.

Transit Passenger Origin Inference

Because smart card readers in the flat-rate buses do not record passengers' boarding stops, it is desired to infer individual boarding location using smart card transaction data. In this section, two primary approaches are presented to achieve this goal. Approximately 50% transit vehicles are equipped with GPS devices in Beijing entry-only AFC system. Therefore, a data fusion method with GPS data, smart card data and GIS data is firstly developed to estimate each bus's arrival time at each stop and infer individual passenger's boarding stop. And then, for those buses without GIS devices, a Bayesian decision tree algorithm is proposed to utilize smart card transaction time and apply Bayesian inference theory to depict the likelihood of each possible boarding stop. In order to expand the usability of proposed Bayesian decision tree algorithm in large-scale datasets, Markov chain optimization is used to reduce the algorithm's computational complexity. Both two transit passenger origin inference algorithms are validated using external data (e.g., on-board survey data and GPS data).

Passenger Origin Inference with GPS Data

In the first step, a GPS-based arrival information inference algorithm is presented to estimate the arrival time for each transit stop, and then, the inferred stop-level arrival time will be matched with the timestamp recorded in AFC system. The temporally closest smart card transaction record will be assigned with each known stop ID. The logic flow chart is demonstrated in Figure 2. The major data processing procedure will be detailed below.

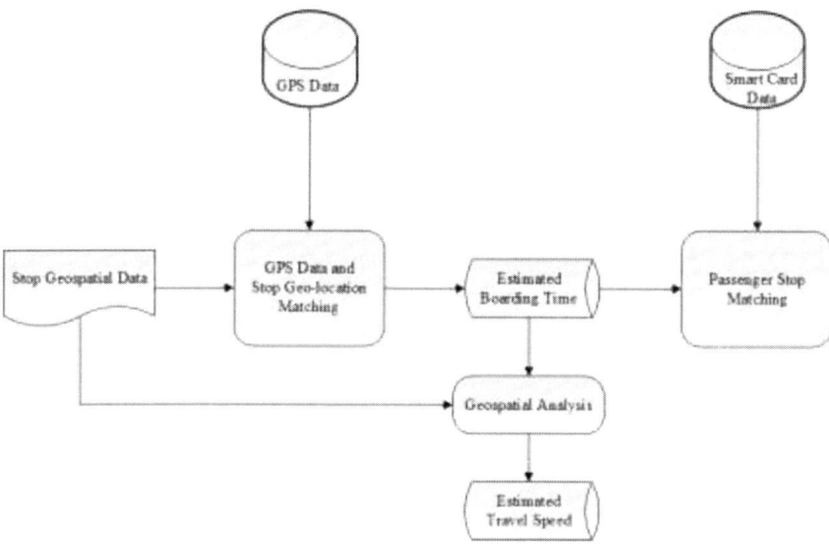

Figure 2. Flow Chart for Passenger Origin Inference with GPS Data.

Bus Arrival Time Extraction

Three primary data sources are involved in the passenger information extraction: vehicle GPS data; transit stop spatial location data; and flat-fare-based smart card transaction data. A transit GIS network contains the geospatial location of each stop for any transit routes. The GPS device mounted in the bus can record each bus's location and timestamp every 30 seconds, but the data quality of collected GPS records is not satisfying: No directional information is recorded in Beijing AVL system; GPS points are off the roadway network due to the satellite signal fluctuation. Data preprocessing is required prior to bus arrival time estimation. A program is written to parse and import raw GPS data into a database in an automatic manner. Key fields of a GPS record are shown in Table 1.

Table 1. Examples of GPS raw data

Vehicle ID	Date time	Latitude	Longitude	Spot speed	Route ID
00034603	2010-04-07 09:28:57	39.73875	116.1355	9.07	00022
00034603	2010-04-07 09:29:27	39.73710	116.1358	14.26	00022
00034603	2010-04-07 09:29:58	39.73592	116.1357	19.63	00022
00034603	2010-04-07 09:30:28	39.73479	116.1357	0	00022
00034603	2010-04-07 09:30:58	39.73420	116.1357	3.52	00022

The first step is to estimate the bus arrival time for each stop by joining GPS data and the stop-level geo-location data. A buffer area can be created around each particular stop for a certain transit route using the GIS software. Within this area, several GPS records are likely to be captured. However, identifying the geospatially closest GPS record to each particular stop is challenging since there could be a certain number of unknown directional GPS records within the specified buffer zone. Thanks to the powerful geospatial analysis function in GIS, each link (i.e., polyline) where each transit stop is located is composed of both start node and end node, and this implies that the directional information for each GPS record is able to infer by comparing the link direction and the direction changes from two consecutive GPS records. With the identified direction, the distance from each GPS point to this particular stop can be calculated, and the timestamp with the minimum distance will be regarded as the bus arrival time at the particular stop. Figure 2 visually demonstrates the above algorithm procedure. Inbound stop represents the physical location of a particular transit stop, and this stop is snapped to a transit link, whose direction is regulated by both a start node and an end node. By comparing the driving direction from GPS records with the link direction, the nearest GPS records to this particular stop can be identified, and marked by the red five-pointed star on the map. The timestamp associated with this five-pointed star will be considered as the arrival time for this inbound stop. The merit of the bus arrival time estimation algorithm lies in its efficiency. Rather than searching all the GPS data to identify the traveling direction for each stop, the proposed algorithm shrinks down the searching area, and filters out those unlikely GPS data. The operation greatly alleviates the computational burden, and is relatively easy to implement in the large-scale datasets, which is particularly critical to process the tremendous amount of datasets within an acceptable time period.

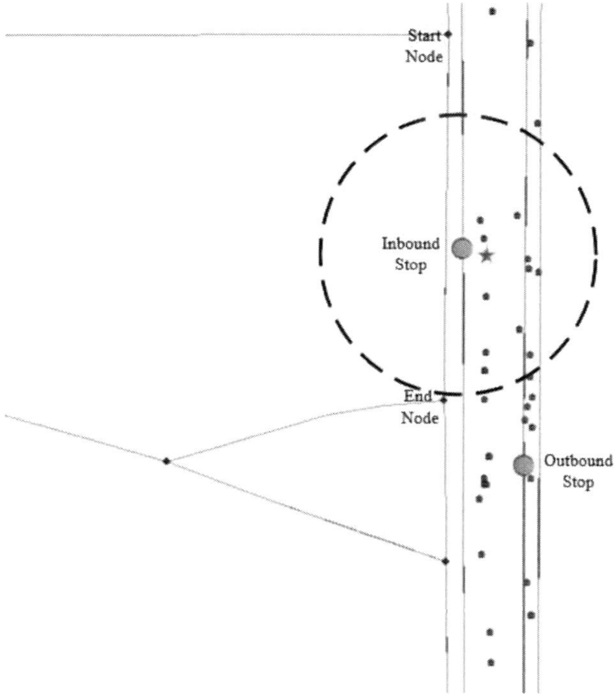

Figure 3. Boarding Time Estimation with GPS Data and Transit Stop Location Data.

Passenger Boarding Location Identification with Smart Card Data

For each smart card data transaction record, the boarding stop can be estimated by matching the recorded timestamp and the identified bus arrival time. As presented in Figure 4, for each smart card transaction record, the transaction time is compared with the inferred bus arrival time at each stop. This record will be assigned to a particular stop where the bus arrival time is the most temporally closed with its transaction time. Since passengers begin to embark the bus at a relative short time interval, this data fusion method is able to capture almost all missing boarding stops.

Bus Arrival Time Table

Vehicle ID	Route ID	Arrival time	Direction	Stop ID	Average Speed
00034603	00022	09:30:28	Inbound	1	19.03
00034603	00022	09:38:02	Inbound	2	24.72

Card ID	Vehicle ID	Route ID	Timestamp	Boarding Stop ID
31158	00034603	00022	09:30:30	1
58934	00034603	00022	09:30:31	1
69782	00034603	00022	09:30:35	1
15678	00034603	00022	09:30:39	1
36789	00034603	00022	09:30:43	1
28948	00034603	00022	09:38:05	2
12304	00034603	00022	09:38:08	2
96347	00034603	00022	09:38:10	2
89635	00034603	00022	09:38:11	2

Smart Card Transaction Table

Figure 4. Boarding Stop Identification with Bus Arrival Time.

In addition, because all the arrival time for all stops of a particular transit route can be estimated, the average travel time between two adjacent stops can be calculated as well. This speed statistics is not only critical for transit performance measures, but also provides prior information for passenger origin inference when GPS data are absent.

Validation

Compared with bus arrival time, door opening time can be more accurately matched with smart card transaction time. This is because each bus may not exactly stop at each transit stop for passenger boarding. The inferred bus arrival time is subject to incur errors when it is used to match with smart card data. To validate the accuracy of the proposed data fusion algorithm for passenger origin inference, on-board transit survey was undertaken to collect bus door opening time and arrival location for each stop of route 651 on January, 13th, 2013. Hand holding GPS devices were used to track the geospatial location of moving buses every 15 seconds. The survey duration was from 8:00 AM to 1: 00 PM, and a total of 75 bus door opening time was manually recorded. These bus door opening time records were then compared with smart card transactions from 417 passengers, and these estimated stops can be considered as the ground-truth data. By comparing the ground-truth data with the results from the proposed GPS data fusion approach, 406 boarding stops were accurately inferred and 11 boarding stops differ from the ground-truth data within one-stop-error range. The proposed algorithm demonstrates its accuracy as high as 97.4%.

Passenger Origin Inference with Smart Card Data

There are still a fair amount of buses without GPS devices, and thus the bus arrival time at each transit stop is not directly measured. However, most passengers scan their cards immediately when boarding and almost all passengers should complete the check-in scan before arriving to the next stop. This indicates that the first passenger's transaction time can be safely assumed as the group of passengers' boarding time at the same stop. The challenge is then to identify the bus location at the moment of the SC transaction so that we can infer the onboard stop for that passenger. However, this is not easy because the SC system for the flat-rate bus does not record bus location. We know the time each transaction occurred on a bus of a particular route under the operation of a particular driver, but nothing else is known from the SC transaction database. Nonetheless, we are able to extract boarding volume changes with time and passengers who made transfers. By mining these data and combining transit route maps, we may be able to accomplish our goal. Therefore, a two-step approach is designed for passenger origin data extraction: smart card data clustering and transit stop recognition. To implement the proposed algorithm in an efficient manner, a Markov Chain based optimization approach is applied to reduce the computational complexity.

Smart Card Data Clustering

Transaction Data Classification

First of all, we need to sort SC transactions by the transit vehicle number. This results in a list of SC transactions in the vehicle for the entire period of operations for each day. During the operational period, the vehicle may have two to ten round-trip runs depending on the round-trip length and roadway condition. At a terminal station, a transit vehicle may take a break or continue running. So there is no obvious signal for the end of a trip (a trip is defined as the journey from one terminus to the other terminus). Meanwhile, there are a varying number of passengers at each stop, including some stops with no passengers.

For stops with several passengers boarding, all transactions can be classified into one group based on interval between their transactions. Thus, the clustered SC transactions can be represented by a time series of check-in passenger volumes at stops as shown in Table 2.

Table 2. Examples of Clustered SC transactions

Transaction Cluster No.	Stop ID	Stop Name	Total Transactions	Transaction Timestamp	Time Difference
1	Unknown	Unknown	18	5:26:36	0:14:26
2	Unknown	Unknown	9	5:41:02	0:03:16
3	Unknown	Unknown	11	5:44:18	0:04:35
4	Unknown	Unknown	27	5:48:53	0:01:00

In Table 2, total transactions indicate the total boarding passengers in one stop; transaction timestamp is recorded as the time when the first passenger boards in this stop, and time difference means the elapsed time between the boarding time at this stop and next stop with boarding passengers. Unlike most entry-only AFC systems in the United States, stop name and ID from each transaction are unknown in Beijing's AFC system. Most buses in service follow the predefined order of stops, however, it is still possible that there is no passenger boarding in a specific stop, and thus two consecutive SC transaction clusters do not necessarily correspond to two physically consecutive stops. Obviously, this further complicates the situation and the algorithm needed is indeed to map each cluster into the corresponding boarding stop ID.

In summary, the smart card data clustering algorithm contains three steps as follows:

Step 1: All transaction data for each bus are sorted by the transaction timestamp in an ascending order.

Step 2: For two consecutive records, if their transaction time difference is within 60 sec, then, these two transactions are included in one cluster; otherwise, another cluster is initiated.

Step 3: If the transaction time difference for two consecutive records is greater than 30 min or driver changing occurs, it is likely that the bus has arrived in terminus, and for this bus, one bus trip has completed. Next record will be the beginning for the next bus trip.

The result of the clustering process is several sequences of clustered transactions. Each sequence may contain one or more trips of the transit vehicle. For particular routes, due to the limited space in terminus or busy transit schedule, bus layover time may be too short to be used as a separation symbol for trips. Such buses may have a very long clustered sequence that makes the pattern discovery process very challenging. Furthermore, unfamiliar passengers or passengers boarding from the check-out doors (this happens for very crowded buses) may take longer than 60 seconds to scan their cards. The delayed transaction may cause cluster assignment errors. Again, this adds extra challenge to the follow-up passenger origin extraction process.

Transaction Cluster Sequence Segmentation

Beijing has a huge transit network with nearly 1,000 routes. It is quite common to see passengers transfer between transit routes. Through transfer activity analysis, we can further segment the clustered transaction sequence into shorter series to reduce the uncertainty in passenger OD estimation (Jang, 2010). Two key principles used in the transfer stop identification are:

(1) We assume the alighting stop in the previous route is spatially and temporally the closest to the boarding stop for the next route. This is reasonable because most passengers choose the closest stop for transit transfer within a short period of time (Chu, 2008). Assume a passenger k makes a transfer from route i to route j within n minutes. If route i is a distance-based-rate bus line or a subway line, then we can identify the transfer station that is also the boarding stop of route j. Even if both routes are flat-rate bus routes, if the transferring location is unique, we can still use the transfer information to identify the transfer bus stop ID and name. In this study, the transfer time duration n is 30 minutes, and the maximum distance between two transfer stops is 300 meters.

(2) We assume that both the alighting time and the boarding time for each particular stop is similar. In this case, we can substitute a passenger boarding stop with another passenger alighting stop. Assume a passenger k makes a transfer from route i to route j. If route j is a subway line, where both its boarding location and time are available, then we can estimate the passenger k's alighting stop of route i, and this alighting stop can be also considered as the boarding stop for those passengers who get on the bus at the same time.

Walk distance between the two stops should be taken into account for inferring the time when the flat-rate bus arrives at the transfer stop. However, several possible boarding stops may exist due to the unknown direction in the flat-rate smart card transaction, and thus additional data mining techniques are needed to find the boarding stop with the maximum likelihood. These data mining techniques will be detailed in the next section.

Based on the identified transfer stops, we can further segment the transaction cluster sequence into shorter cluster series. Each series is bounded by either the termini or the identified bus stops. The segmented series of transaction clusters will be used as the input for the subsequent transit stop inference algorithm.

Data Mining for Transit Stop Recognition

Bayesian Decision Tree Inference

If we treat each segmented series of transaction cluster as an unknown pattern, this unknown pattern can be considered as a sample of the sequential stops on the bus route. If every stop has boarding passengers, this unknown pattern is identical to the known bus stop sequence. Also, since distance and speed limit between stops are known, travel time between stops is highly predictable if there is no traffic jam. In reality, however, there may have varying distribution of passengers boarding at any given stop and roadway congestion may cost unpredictable delays. Therefore, the unknown pattern recognition is a very challenging issue. Once the unknown pattern is recognized, the boarding stop for any passenger becomes clear.

Bayesian decision tree algorithm is one of the widely used data mining techniques for pattern recognition (Janssens et al., 2006). Each node in the Bayesian decision tree is connected through Bayesian conditional probability, and the entire tree is constructed directionally from the root node to the leaf nodes. Applying this technique to the current problem, we can represent the known starting stop as the root. if we denote the current boarding stop ID at time step k as S_k, and at time step k+1, the next boarding stop ID as S_{k+1}, according to Bayesian inference theory (Bayes and Price, 1763), S_{k+1} can be calculated as:

$$S_{k+1} = \arg\max_j (\Pr(S_{k+1} = j \mid S_1, S_2 ... S_k)) \quad (1)$$

where $\Pr(S_{k+1} \mid S_1, S_2 ... S_k)$ =conditional probability of the next boarding stop being S_{k+1}, given the previous boarding stop sequence $S_1, S_2 ... S_k$.

A Bayesian decision tree represents many possible known patterns. We need to compute the probability for each known pattern to match the unknown pattern. By further observation, we can find due to the nature of transit route, the probability of passengers boarding at S_{k+1} at time step k+1 is only related to whether the last boarding stop was S_k at time step k. That is because if the transaction time and corresponding bus location for SC transaction cluster k is known, the next SC transaction cluster k+1 only relies on how fast the bus travels during the time period between SC transaction clusters k and k+1. In this case, a SC transaction series can be recognized as a Markov chain process. Markov chain is a stochastic process with the property that the next state only relies on the current state. Therefore, S_{k+1} can be rewritten as:

$$S_{k+1} = \arg\max_j(\Pr(S_{k+1} = j \mid S_1, S_2 ... S_k)) = \arg\max_j(\Pr(S_{k+1} = j \mid S_k = i)) \quad \text{subject to } i < j \tag{2}$$

The single-step Markov transition probability is defined as $\Pr(S_{k+1} = j \mid S_k = i)$, also denoted as p_{ij}, with i, j being the stop IDs. Without losing generality, we assume the bus is moving outbound with an increasing trend of stop ID toward the destination. Then the transition probability matrix Π can be simplified as:

$$\Pi = \begin{pmatrix} p_{11} & p_{12} \cdots & p_{1n} \\ p_{21} & p_{22} \cdots & p_{2n} \\ \vdots & \vdots & \vdots \\ p_{(n-1)1} & p_{(n-1)2} \cdots & p_{(n-1)n} \\ p_{n1} & p_{n2} \cdots & p_{nn} \end{pmatrix} = \begin{pmatrix} 1 - \sum_{i=2}^{n} p_{1i} & p_{12} \cdots & p_{1n} \\ 0 & 1 - \sum_{i=2}^{n} p_{2i} \cdots & p_{2n} \\ \vdots & \vdots & \vdots \\ 0 & 0 \dots & p_{(n-1)n} \\ 0 & 0 \dots & 1 \end{pmatrix} \tag{3}$$

where n=the total number of stops for the bus route. This transition probability matrix plays a vital role in determining the potential stop ID for the next time step.

Bayesian Decision Tree Inference

To recognize the unknown pattern, it is critical to develop a measure to quantify p_{ij}, the possibility of next boarding stop being stop j conditioned on the previous boarding stop being i. The higher p_{ij} is, the more likely the next SC transaction cluster corresponds to boarding passengers at stop j. In other words, p_{ij} represents the probability for the next SC transaction cluster timestamp being the bus boarding time at stop j. That is to say, the boarding time in stop j for cluster k+1 can be predicted based on the travel distance from stop i to stop j and average bus speed. Then, the calculated time can be used as an indicator to compare with the real transaction timestamp for cluster k+1. From this point, the average speed between stops i and j will be a key variable. If the timestamp for cluster k is t_k, and that for cluster k+1 is t_{k+1}, then, the bus travel time from time step k to time step k+1 is $t_{k+1} - t_k$, and the stop distance between stop j and stop i is D_{ij}, then, the average bus travel speed V_{ij} can be expressed as:

$$V_{ij} = \frac{D_{ij}}{t_{k+1} - t_k} \quad (4)$$

where V_{ij} is a random variable depending on the traffic condition at the moment. V_{ij} is considered to be normally distributed, and its probability density function can be adopted to quantifying p_{ij}.

In the speed normal distribution, the mean travel speed μ_{ij} and standard deviation σ_{ij} can be calculated from all buses with GPS devices in the same route. Under this circumstance, the boarding time for each stop can be inferred by matching GPS data and stop location information. Using the inferred boarding time difference and distance between stop i and stop j, we can calculate the mean travel speed μ_{ij} and standard deviation σ_{ij} as a priori information. It is noteworthy that the speed mean and standard deviation are not dependent on GPS data, but can be also obtained by other data sources such as distance-based-rate SC transaction data. A sensitivity analysis further demonstrates the algorithm's robustness even with different speed data sources.

Then, the transition probability can be reformulated as:

$$\begin{aligned} p_{ij} &= \Pr(S_{k+1} = j \mid S_k = i) \\ &= \int_{z_{ij}-\Delta}^{z_{ij}+\Delta} \frac{1}{\sqrt{2\pi}} \exp(-z^2/2)dz = \frac{1}{\sqrt{2\pi}} \exp(-z_{ij}^2/2) \cdot 2\Delta, \end{aligned} \tag{5}$$

where $Z_{ij} = \frac{V_{ij} - \mu_{ij}}{\sigma_{ij}}$, which is the standardized travel speed between stop j and stop i, Δ is a small increase value for travel speed, and it will not impact the algorithm result, since this is a common term for each transition probability. In practice, to avoid the fast growth of Bayesian decision tree, the transition probability can be bounded by a minimum probability to eliminate those unlikely stops during calculation.

Each element in transition matrix can be quantified in the same way as shown in Equation (5). With the complete transition matrix, the unknown pattern of SC transaction series can be recognized as:

$$\begin{aligned} &[S_{k+1}, S_k, S_{k-1}, ..., S_1] \\ &= \arg\max_{S_1...S_{k+1}} \Pr(S_{k+1}, S_k, S_{k-1}, ..., S_1) \\ &= \arg\max_{S_1...S_{k+1}} \left(\Pr(S_{k+1} \mid S_k, S_{k-1}, ..., S_1)\Pr(S_k, S_{k-1}, ..., S_1)\right) \\ &= \arg\max_{S_1...S_{k+1}} \left(\Pr(S_{k+1} \mid S_k)\Pr(S_k \mid S_{k-1}) \cdots \Pr(S_2 \mid S_1)\right) \\ &= \arg\max_{S_1...S_{k+1}} (\prod_{n=1}^{k} \Pr(S_{n+1} = j \mid S_n = i)) \\ &= \arg\max_{S_1...S_{k+1}} (\sqrt[k+1]{\prod_{n=1}^{k} \Pr(S_{n+1} = j \mid S_n = i)}) \\ &= \arg\max_{S_1...S_{k+1}} (\overline{P}(k+1)) \end{aligned} \tag{6}$$

Here, $\overline{P}(k+1) = \sqrt[k+1]{\prod_{n=1}^{k} \Pr(S_{n+1} = j \mid S_n = i)}$ denotes the geometric mean probability of passengers boarding stop sequence at time step k+1. It is also the probability for the identified stop sequence to match the unknown pattern.

Algorithm Implementation and Optimization

Implementation

As mentioned in the previous sections, due to the nature of transaction data, several issues need to be addressed in the process of Markov chain based Bayesian decision tree algorithm:

1. Direction identification

Beijing transit AFC system doesn't log the travel direction information for each route. We need to determine whether the bus is traveling inbound or outbound before algorithm execution. The solution is that we construct two Bayesian decision trees in each direction. Then the probability of the most likely stop sequence from each of trees will be compared and the one with the highest path probability wins.

2. Outlier removal

As mentioned in the Smart Card Data Clustering section, in some cases, the delayed transactions impact the accuracy of clustering algorithm, and these abnormal transactions are also labeled as outliers. The principal difficulty is that two inconsistent SC transactions by timestamp that should be classified in one cluster may be read separately, and thus, the latter will be classified as another cluster for the next stop. For instance, at a particular stop, if one passenger boarded the bus and paid the fare at 8:00 AM, another passenger swiped his smart card to alight at 8:10 AM. Due to the relative large transaction timestamp gap, the second transaction will be assigned to another cluster. In this case, the boarding stop ID will be misidentified.

The strategy used to remove these outliers is that there exists a probability that a passenger may retain in the same stop. If the previous stop ID is defined as i, the number of total stops in each possible direction is denoted as N, and the probability that a passenger stay at stop i in the next time step can be expressed as:

$$p_{ii} = 1 - \sum_{j=i+1}^{j \le N} p_{ij} \tag{7}$$

The probability is able to better depict the situation where passengers may delay a certain period to swipe their smart cards during boarding.

3. Bus trip detection

The journey begins from the initial bus stop to the terminus is defined as a bus trip. The bus terminus is designed for bus turning, layover, and driver change. It is also the starting stop on the bus timetable. However, in Beijing's transit network, some bus termini are located in the busy street or have limited space. Hence, buses using these termini have to begin their next trip in a short time period without causing an obstruction. This is a challenging issue in the procedure of passenger origin inference, since the initial stop (root node) in Bayesian decision tree may be misidentified if the bus trip is mistakenly detected. The solution to this issue is to model the travel time probability of each transaction cluster series. As indicated in the transaction cluster sequence segmentation section, a transaction cluster sequence can be segmented by several series using aforementioned spatiotemporal transfer relationships. Each identified series is bounded by possible inferred stops, by calculating the travel time for multiple combinations of inferred stops, and comparing with the actual time difference, we are able to determine the existence of a bus trip based on the highest probability. Figure 5 demonstrates the procedure of identifying a bus trip.

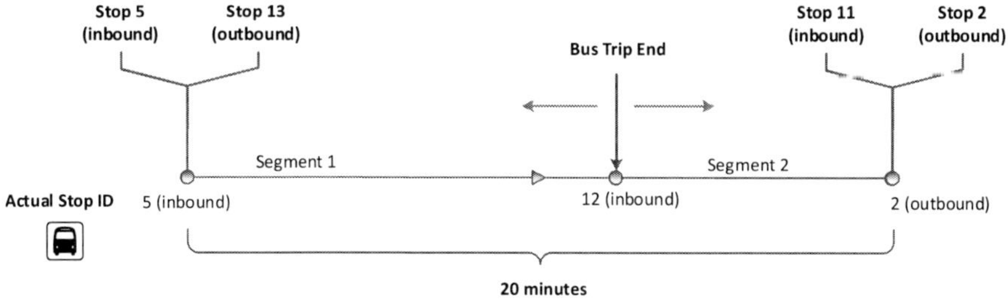

Figure 5. Bus Trip Identification.

As presented in Figure 5, the starting point and ending point of the series can be identified by several possible stops in different directions, and the duration of this transaction cluster series is known as 20 minutes. A variety of trips may exist for this transaction cluster sequence:

Trip 1: The bus travels from the 5th inbound stop to the 11th inbound stop.
Trip 2: The bus travels from the 5th inbound stop to the 2nd outbound stop.
Trip 3: The bus travels from the 13th outbound stop to the 11th inbound stop.
Trip 4: The bus travels from the 13th outbound stop to the 2nd outbound stop.

The maximum and minimum travel time for any trip can be obtained through GPS data or distance-based buses. In addition, the maximum bus layover time can be assumed as 30 minutes. According to the central limit theorem, bus travel time in a known road segment should follow normal distribution, and therefore, we can compute the probability of each scenario, and choose the trip with the maximum probability. If the travel time from stop i to stop j is denoted as t_{ij}, and the probability density function of t_{ij} is defined as:

$$p(t_{ij}) = \frac{1}{\sqrt{2\pi\sigma_{ij}^2}} \exp(-\frac{(t_{ij} - \mu_{ij})^2}{2\sigma_{ij}^2}) dt_{ij} \tag{8}$$

where μ_{ij} is the average travel time from stop i to stop j, and σ_{ij} is the standard deviation of travel time from stop i to stop j. If the maximum and minimum travel time (plus maximum and minimum bus layover time) between stop i to stop j are $\max(t_{ij})$ and $\min(t_{ij})$ respectively, then the 95% confidence interval of travel time can be further expressed as:

$$[\mu_{ij} - 1.96\sigma_{ij}, \mu_{ij} + 1.96\sigma_{ij}] = [\min(t_{ij}), \max(t_{ij})] \tag{9}$$

The probability density function of t_{ij} can be rewritten as:

$$p(t_{ij}) = \frac{1}{\sqrt{2\pi(\frac{\max(t_{ij}) - \min(t_{ij})}{3.92})^2}} \exp(-\frac{(t_{ij} - \frac{\max(t_{ij}) + \min(t_{ij})}{2})^2}{2(\frac{\max(t_{ij}) - \min(t_{ij})}{3.92})^2}) dt_{ij} \tag{10}$$

Each probability for the above four trips can be calculated as 0.54, 0.87, 0.0003 and 0. Therefore, the transaction cluster sequence starts at the 5th inbound stop, and ends at the 2nd outbound stop, and thus a terminus should exist during this trip. This result matched with the actual bus trip. Bayesian decision tree algorithm can be further utilized to infer other uncertain stops within this identified bus trip.

Computational Performance Optimization

Although we illustrated the mathematical form for Markov chain based Bayesian decision tree in theory, this algorithm presented above has not been applied in the real dataset. Cooper (1990) has proven Bayesian decision tree algorithm a NP (Non-deterministic Polynomial)-hard problem, which means that this algorithm cannot be solved in a polynomial time. Conventional approach to calculate the path probability for all the potential boarding stop sequences is computationally expensive, especially for the long sequences. To better explain this challenge, an example is shown as follows:

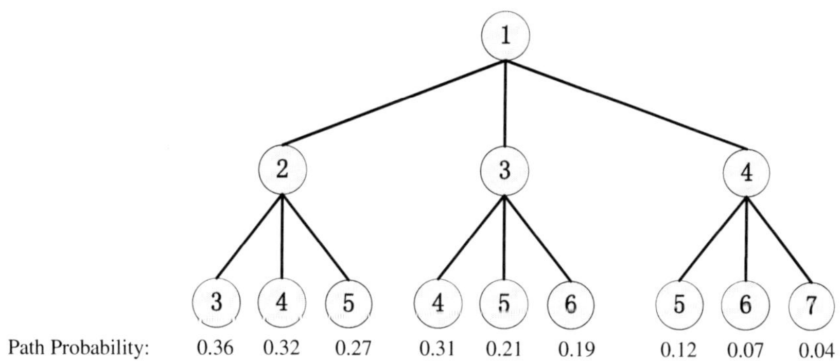

Figure 6. A Bayesian Decision Tree Algorithm Example.

Assume the initial boarding stop is 1. The potential stops in the next step could be stop 2, stop 3, or stop 4 because they are all in the reachable range. Assuming that the situations are similar for the remaining stops, a decision tree is fully established. The traditional exhaustive search is to traverse each potential path, and select the maximum probability. Based on this method, we need to calculate the path probability nine times. This implies that the number of paths to be calculated increases exponentially as the time step increases. However, at the time step 3, there are two or more paths ending with stop 3, 4 and 5. Before carrying on the computation in the next time step, we can compare the probability of the paths with the same ending stop, and choose the maximum one, which is also called the partial best path.

In the time step 3, only the following five paths are selected 1->2->3, 1->2->4,1->2->5,1->3->6, and 1->4->7. Recall that the Markov Chain model states that the probability of current state given a previous state sequence depends only on the previous state. Hence, five paths calculated in time step 3 guarantees the most probable paths in time step 4 without extra computations of other paths. According to Equation (11), we can express the optimized procedure in mathematics as:

$$\overline{P}(k+1) = \max_{i,j}(\overline{P}(k)(\sqrt[k+1]{\Pr(S_{k+1} = j \mid S_k = i)})) \qquad (11)$$

We can now calculate the probability at each time step recursively until the end of the route. Computing the probability in this way is far less computational expensive than calculating the probabilities for all sequences. If we denoted the total stops for a specific route as n, and the SC transactions are classified in m clusters, which correspond to m time steps in Bayesian decision trees, then the computational complexity for the exhaustive approach can be written as $O(m^n)$. While using the optimized algorithm, the computational complexity is only $O(mn)$. With the optimization, the algorithm can be solved in a finite time, and can be efficiently applied in reality.

Validation

By installing GPS receivers on flat-rate buses, we can collect the geospatial information and spot speed data in a real-time manner. There are approximately 50% buses equipped with GPS devices in Beijing, and GPS data are updated every 30 seconds. These data provide the opportunity to validate the Markov-chain based Bayesian decision tree algorithm developed in this study for passenger origin data extraction. GPS coordinates and timestamp can be used to determine bus boarding and alighting location and time. First, the geographical feature of bus stops and consecutive GPS records for each bus are joined using latitude and longitude coordinates. Then, by matching the passenger check-in time in the SC transaction database, the boarding stop ID can be associated with each transaction. Since the inferred stop ID using GPS data have been validated using the bus on-board survey method, and can be considered as the 'ground truth' data for the comparison purpose.

In this section, the Markov chain based Bayesian decision tree algorithm is first validated using GPS data for route 22, and then, several sensitivity analyses are conducted to investigate impacts of different parameter settings in Bayesian decision tree. Finally, a computational complexity experiment is also included at the end of this section.

Algorithm Validation

Flat-rate based route 22 was selected to infer unknown boarding location using Markov chain based Bayesian decision tree algorithm, and GPS data associated with route 22 was also collected to verify the result. The SC transaction data and GPS data are all recorded on April 7, 2010. The minimum stop probability is defined as 0.05. If a stop whose transition probability is less than 0.05, then this stop will be abandoned. Route 22 contains a total of 34 inbound and outbound stops as shown in Figure 7.

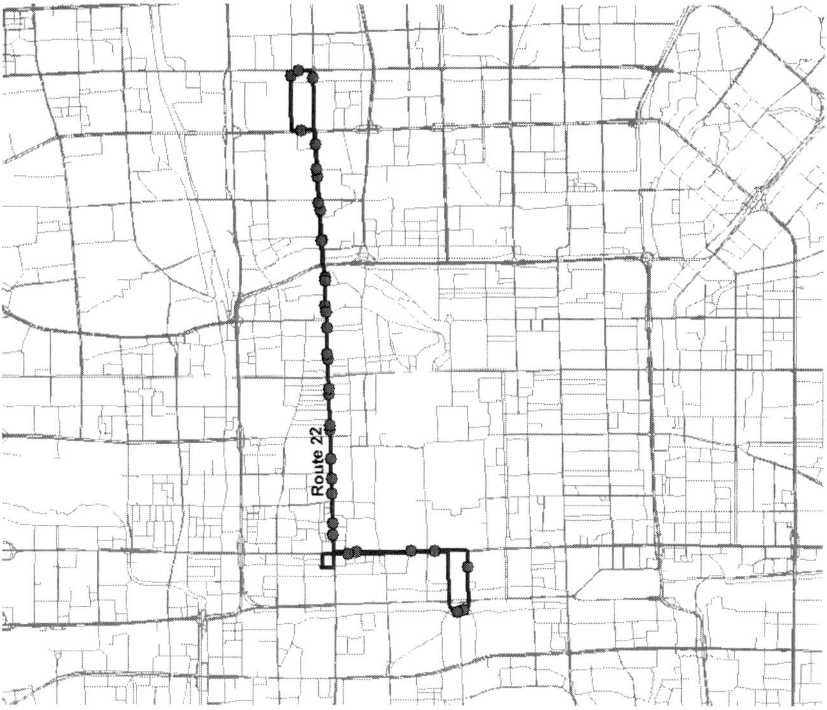

Figure 7. Route 22 in Beijing Transit Network.

The algorithm results are listed as in Table 3 and Figure 8. In Table 3, there are a total of 12,675 SC transactions mapped with GPS data for Route

22. Error is defined as the stop ID difference (two stops that are adjacent to each other should have consecutive IDs) between the ground truth stop based on GPS data and the inferred stop using the proposed algorithm. For Route 22, 95% passenger boarding stops were deducted by the proposed algorithm. 55.8% of results perfectly match with the stops inferred by GPS accurately. There are 11,645 recognized boarding stops within three-stop distance away from the actual boarding stop, accounting for approximately 96.7% of the total identified records or 91.6% of total records.

Table 3. Results of Bayesian Decision Tree Algorithm for Route 22 Based on GPS Speed

Route 22	Number of records	Accumulated percentage in inferred records	Accumulated percentage in total records
Stop ID error<1	7062	58.6%	55.8%
Stop ID error<2	10371	86.1%	81.8%
Stop ID error<3	11341	94.2%	89.5%
Stop ID error<4	11645	96.7%	91.9%
Total	12043	N/A	97.9%

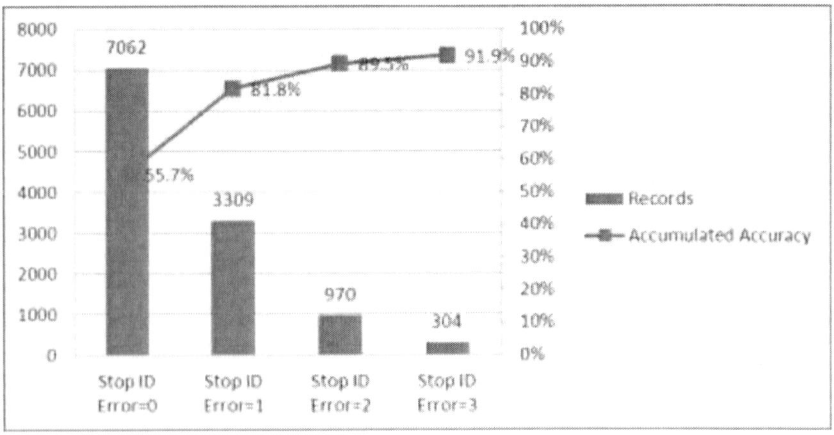

Figure 8. Bayesian Decision Tree Algorithm Accuracy for Route 22 based on GPS Speed.

The results are very encouraging. In Beijing's transit network, the error within three stops is acceptable for transit planning level study, since these stops are mostly affiliated with the same traffic analysis zone (TAZ) due to the high transit network density.

Sensitivity Analysis

1. Source of travel speed calculation

Recall that in computing the transition matrix, mean travel speed μ and standard deviation σ were extracted from GPS data. However, there are still many flat-rate routes without GPS devices. To understand how the algorithm result changes when the travel speed mean and standard deviation are inaccurate, a sensitivity analysis is carried out for this purpose. Table 4 and Figure 9 show the results when the mean and standard deviation of travel speed are retrieved from the distance-based fare routes, and these routes share common stops with the "no-GPS" flat-fare route. Because both boarding stop and alighting stop are known in the distance-based fare buses, we are still able to extract the mean and standard deviation of travel speed between adjacent stops for transition matrix construction.

Table 4. Results of Bayesian Decision Tree Algorithm for Route 22 Based on Speed from Distance-based Fare Routes

Route 22	Number of records	Accumulated percentage in inferred records	Accumulated percentage in total records
Stop ID error<1	6841	58.5%	54%
Stop ID error<2	10319	88.2%	81.4%
Stop ID error<3	11296	96.6%	89.1%
Stop ID error<4	11509	98.4%	90.8%
Total	11694	N/A	92.2%

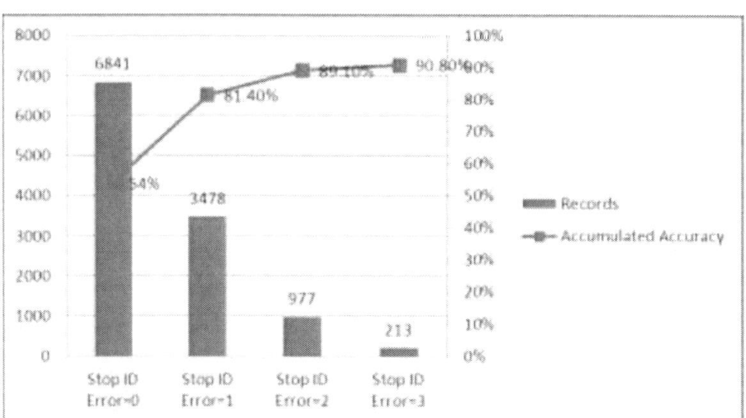

Figure 9. Bayesian Decision Tree Algorithm Accuracy for Route 22 Based on Speed from Distance-based Fare Routes.

Different data sources only slightly influence the percentage of inferred stops. 92.2% boarding stops can be estimated using the speed generated from distance-based fare routes, and the accuracy within three-stop error is 90.8%. The result indicates the proposed algorithm is not sensitive to the travel speed, even without GPS data, we are still able to correctly identify passenger boarding stops using other data sources. This is not surprising, because in normal distribution, mean and standard only influence the shape for probability density function, as long as we make a reasonable assumption for bus travel speed calculation, the algorithm results will not fluctuate significantly.

2. Minimum stop probability

Minimum stop probability plays a vital role to impact both the accuracy and efficiency of the proposed algorithm. A too high threshold may eliminate possible boarding stop candidates, and a too low threshold may consume additional computation resources. In this sensitivity analysis, a different minimum stop probability is set as 0.1, which means if the calculated transition probability of a particular stop is lower than 0.1, and then this stop is considered as an unlikely boarding stop. The comparison result is presented in Table 5 and Figure 10.

When the minimum stop probability increases, less boarding stops can be inferred using the proposed algorithm. In addition, the inferred boarding stops are less accurate compared with the ones with minimum stop probability as 0.05. This is a reasonable result since a rigorous probability threshold may limit the prorogation of errors. However, a trade-off exists between algorithm accuracy and efficiency.

Table 5. Results of Bayesian Decision Tree Algorithm for Route 22 with Minimum Stop Probability as 0.1

Route 22	Number of Records	Accumulated Percentage in inferred records	Accumulated Percentage in total records
Stop ID error<1	6011	55.2%	47.4%
Stop ID error<2	9157	84.0%	72.2%
Stop ID error<3	10139	93.1%	80.0%
Stop ID error<4	10589	97.2%	83.5%
Total	10894	N/A	85.9%

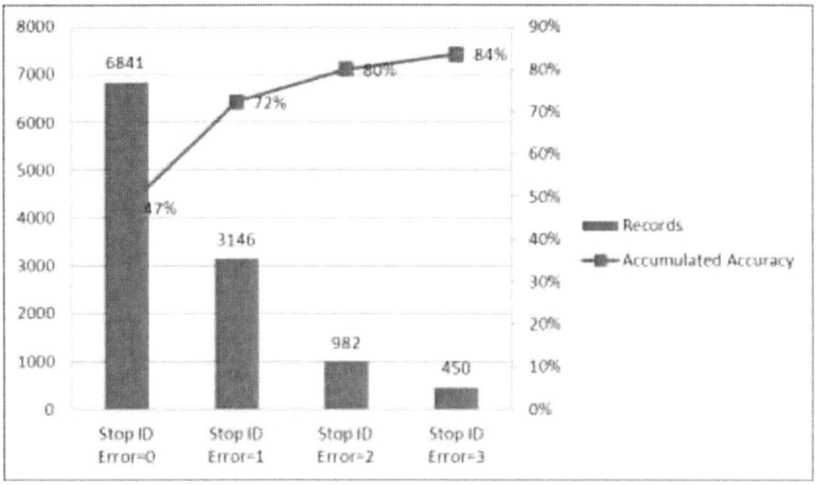

Figure 10. Bayesian Decision Tree Algorithm Accuracy for Route 22 with Minimum Stop Probability as 0.1.

3. Computational complexity comparison

As mentioned in the algorithm optimization section, the computational complexity should be also taken into account when the proposed algorithm is implemented in a large-scale transit network. To compare the algorithm efficiency between the basic Bayesian decision tree algorithm (Basic BDC) and the Markov chain based Bayesian decision tree algorithm (Markov-chain BDC), seven transit routes with an increasing number of total stops are tested. 10,000 smart card transactions for each route on April, 7, 2010 are used for comparison purposes. The experimental result is listed in table 6 and figure 11.

Table 6. Computation Complexity Comparison between Basic and Markov-chain Based Bayesian Decision Tree Algorithms

Route ID	Number of stops	Running time for Basic BDC (milliseconds)	Running time for Markov-chain BDC(milliseconds)
00616	23	3798	493740
00647	36	4890	674820
00005	53	7747	937387
00839	66	17082	1947348
00355	74	21071	2486378
00646	80	23979	4556010
00603	86	29114	5560774

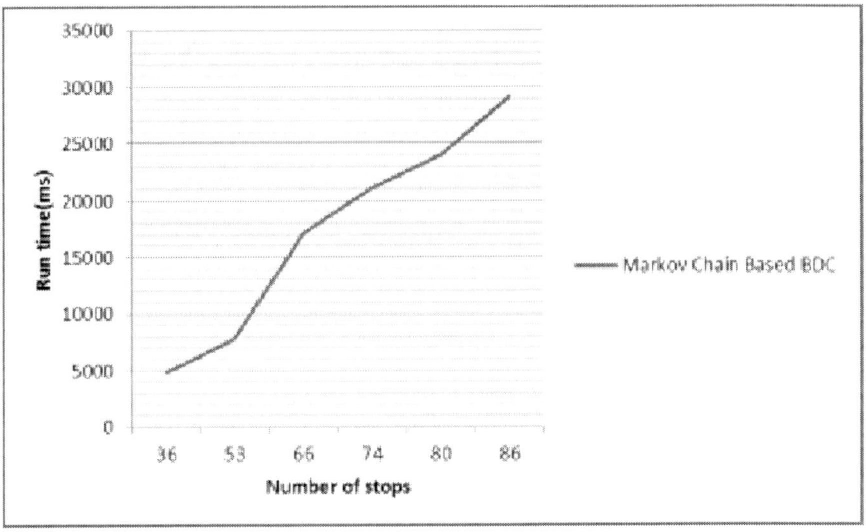

Figure 11. Markov Chain based Bayesian Decision Tree Algorithm Run Time Analysis.

The Markov chain based BDC algorithm can save a significant amount of run time compared with the Basic BDC algorithm. The average performance gains can achieve to 142 times faster than the basic algorithm. This is because most of the redundant calculation steps have been already excluded using Markov chain property.

CONCLUSION

Different from most entry-only AFC systems in other countries, Beijing's AFC system does not record boarding location information when passengers embark the buses and swipe their smart cards. This creates challenges for passenger OD estimation.

This study aims to tackle this issue. With further investigations on SC transactions data, we proposed a Markov chain based Bayesian decision tree algorithm to infer passengers boarding stops. This algorithm is based on Bayesian inference theory, and the normal distribution of travel speed between adjacent stops is used to depict the randomness of passenger boarding stops. Both the mean and the standard deviation can be obtained from GPS data or distance-based fare routes. Moreover, stationary Markov chain property is also incorporated to further reduce the computational complexity of the algorithm to a linear load. The optimized algorithm is proven its accuracy using the SC transaction data.

This algorithm can be improved in various ways; for instance, the algorithm does not perform well under the circumstance that the travel speed between adjacent stops is not distinct, i.e., the travel speed probability calculated for each stop is similar. The potential countermeasure for this issue is to incorporate heterogeneity, e.g., the accessibility of a subway station or a central business district (CBD) for each transit stop.

In summary, the Markov chain based Bayesian decision tree algorithm provides both effective and efficient data mining approach for passenger origin data extraction. It sets up a great foundation to mine transit passenger ODs from the SC transaction data for transit system planning and operations.

ACKNOWLEDGMENTS

The authors would like to appreciate the funding support from the National Natural Science Foundation of China (51408019) and the Fundamental Research Funds for the Central Universities. All data used for this study were provided by Beijing Transportation Research Center (BTRC). We are grateful to BTRC for their data supports.

REFERENCES

Bayes, Thomas; Price, Mr. An essay towards solving a problem in the coctrine of chances, *Philosophical Transactions of the Royal Society of London* 53 (0): 370–418, 1763.

Beijing Transportation Research Center, Beijing transportation smart card usage survey, Research Report. 2010.

Beijing Transportation Research Center, the 4th Beijing Comprehensive Transport Survey Summary Report, Jan. 2012.

Chen, J., 2009. Research on travel demand analysis of urban public transportation based on smart card data information, Ph.D. dissertation, Tongji University.

Chu, K. K. A. and Chapleau, R., Enriching archived smart card transaction data for transit demand modeling, *Transportation Research Record:*

Journal of the Transportation Research Board, Vol. 2063, 2008, pp. 63-72.

Chu, K.K. and Chapleau, R. Augmenting transit trip characterization and travel behavior comprehension: multiday location-stamped smart card transactions. *Transportation Research Record: Journal of the Transportation Research Board*, No. 2183, Transportation Research Board of the National Academies, Washington, DC, 2010, pp.29–40.

Cooper, G. F., The computational complexity of probabilistic inference using Bayesian belief networks, *Artificial Intelligence*, Vol. 42, 1990, pp. 393-405.

Farzin, J. M., Constructing an automated bus Origin-Destination matrix using farecard and Global Positioning System data in Sao Paulo, Brazil, *Transportation Research Record: Journal of the Transportation Research Board*, Vol. 2072, 2008, pp. 30-37.

Federal Highway Administration, Travel Time Reliabiliy: Making it there on time, all the itme, 2006. Accessed on line at: http://ops.fhwa.dot.gov /publications/tt_reliability/, on Apr. 18th, 2013.

Furth, P. G., Hemily, B., Muller, T. H. J., and Strathman, J. G., TCRP report 113: Using archived AVL-APC data to improve transit performance and management, Transportation Research Board, 2006.

Gao, L.X. and Wu, J. P., An algorithm for mining passenger flow information from smart card data, *Journal of Beijing University of Posts and Telecommunications*, Jun. 2011, vol. 34, No.3, 2011, pp. 94-97.

ICF consulting, Center for urban transportation research, Nelson/Nygaard, ESTC. Strategies for Increasing the Effectiveness of Commuter Benefits Programs. TCRP report 87, Transportation Research Board, 2003.

Jang, W, Travel time and transfer analysis using transit smart card data, *Transportation Research Record: Journal of the Transportation Research Board*, Vol. 2144, 2010, pp.142–149.

Janssens, D., Wets, W., Brijs, T., Vanhoof, K., Arentze, T., Timmermans, H., Integrating Bayesian networks and decision trees in a sequential rule-based transportation model, *European Journal of Operational Research*, Vol. 175, Issue 1, 2006, pp. 16-34.

Kittelson & Associates, Inc., Urbitran, Inc. LKC Consulting Services, Inc., Morpace International, Inc., Queensland University of Technology, and Nakanishi, Y., TCRP Report 88, A guidebook for developing a transit performacne-measurement system, Transportation Research Board, National Research Council, Washington, D.C., 2003.

Lou, Y., Zhang, C., Zheng, Y., Xie Xing, Wang, W., and Huang, Y., Map-matching for low-sampling-rate GPS trajectories, Proceedings of the 17th ACM SIGSPATIAL International Conference on Advances in Geographic Information Systems, pp. 352-361, 2009.

Ma, X., McCormack, E., Wang, Y., Processing Commercial GPS Data to Develop a Web-Based Truck Performance Measures Program, *Transportation Research Record: Journal of the Transportation Research Board*. Vol.2246, 2011, pp.92-100.

Ma, X., Wang, Y., Feng, C., and Liu, J. Transit smart card data mining for passenger origin information extraction. *Journal of Zhejiang University Science C*,, Vol. 13, No. 10, 2013, pp. 750-760.

McKenzie, B. and Rapino, M. Commuting in United States: 2009, American Community Survey Reports. Accessed on line at: http://www.census.gov /prod/2011pubs/acs-15.pdf, on Oct. 7th, 2012.

Texas Transportation Institute, 2005 urban mobility report, Texas A&M University, 2005.

Zhou, T., Zhai C., and Gao Z., Approaching bus OD matrices based on data reduced from bus IC cards. *Urban Transport of China*, vol. 5, no.3, 2007, pp. 48-52.

In: Data Mining
Editor: Harold L. Capri
ISBN: 978-1-63463-738-1

Chapter 2

KNOWLEDGE EXTRACTION FROM AN AUTOMATED FORMATIVE EVALUATION BASED ON ODALA APPROACH USING THE WEKA TOOL?

Farida Bouarab-Dahmani[1]* and Razika Tahi[2]#
[1]The Computer Science Department, FGEI Faculty,
University of Tizi-Ouzou, Tizi-Ouzou, Algeria
[2]The Laboratory for the Electrification of Industrial Enterprises,
Department of Economics, University of Boumerdes, Boumerdes, Algeria

ABSTRACT

Differentiation between learners, adapted and personalized learning are interesting research directions on technology for human learning today. This issue leads to the design of educational systems integrating strategies for learners' monitoring to assist each by evaluating his knowledge and skills in one hand and detecting and analyzing his errors and obstacles in the other hand. In this respect, formative evaluation is the process used to capture data on the strengths and weaknesses of a learner. These data, to be useful, must be objectively analyzed so that it can be used to manage the following sessions. There are different data mining tools using different algorithms for data analysis and knowledge

* farida.bd2011@Yahoo.fr
# raztahi@Yahoo.fr

extraction. Can we use these tools in computer based systems? In such cases, is it possible to directly use a variety of general-purpose algorithms for learning data analysis? We discuss in this paper a learning cycle that can be a learning session with feedback loop integrating formative evaluation followed by knowledge extraction process using data mining algorithms. Our experiments, presented in this work, shows a set of tests, about the exploration of learners' errors, obtained from a self e-learning by doing tool for the algorithmic domain. We used the data mining algorithms implemented in the Weka tool: the C4.5 algorithm for classification, A Priori one for association rules deduction and K-Means for clustering. The results given by these experiments have proved the interest of classification and clustering as implemented in Weka. However, the A priori algorithm gives in some cases results difficult to interpret so that it needs a specific optimization to get adequate frequents detection.

Keywords: educational data mining, formative assessment, A Priori algorithm, C4.5 algorithm, K-means clustering algorithm, the Weka tool

1. INTRODUCTION

Educational data mining (Romero, C. and Ventura, S., 2007) is an area of research where appropriate methodological research and technical means are experienced to produce useful knowledge from different types of data (marks, errors, data on the learner, log files ...). These data can be produced by any kind of learning: face to face learning, e-learning or even blended leaning.

Learners' differentiation and adapting learning is basic for competency-based approach that is very discussed nowadays in educational science. The value of a competency-based approach in our new world of global economy and advanced technologies is obvious. However, mistrust and reluctance of teachers and staff, often observed when it comes to the application of this approach in the field, are justified by the difficulty in assessing skills. In addition, this new approach is individual oriented monitoring, which requires more work for everyone in the educational institutions.

With the introduction of the LMD (**L**icense, **M**aster **D**octorate) system in Algerian universities, for example, the competency-based approach have to be applied by individually tracking each student. However, this is not a possible objective with the large number of students which makes this learners' differentiation a tedious task for every faculty member.

The study proposed in this chapter discusses the possible add-ons of data mining tools to computer based learning systems that enhance competency based pedagogies, to get adaptive learning. We are particularly interested in data mining algorithms for knowledge extraction from data given by a formative and automated evaluation based on learners' errors integrated in the ODALA approach. This one is developed and evaluated in our previous works (Bouarab-Dahmani F., 2010) (Bouarab-Dahmani F. et al., 2011). Among, the data mining algorithms, considered in this study, we have: the C4.5 (with the J48 implementation) for classification, A Priori algorithms for associative rules deduction and K-means for clustering.

First, we will give an overview about the ODALA approach and data mining technology. After that, in the third section, we present our tests on mining learning data using some algorithms implemented in the Weka Tool. After that, in the fourth point, we discuss the tests results and data mining implementation in a CEHL. The conclusion is a synthesis about our contribution and the possible research perspective of the presented work.

2. Data Mining and ODALA Approach

Personalization in **c**omputer **e**nvironments for **h**uman **l**earning (CEHL) is possible by the implementation of strategies defined to monitor and assist the learner, based on a recurrent and continuous evaluation of learner's knowledge. Formative evaluation is then a recommended tool used to capture data on the strengths and weaknesses of a learner during a given period. This data can't easily help the decision staff without an objective analysis to get useful knowledge for learning management. However, these analysis processes are always programming time consuming to be integrating to each CEHL system. For that, the use already existing data mining tools seems interesting, but which algorithm? Which tool or library? For what kind of input data and learning management objectives?

Data mining is a field at the intersection of statistics and information technology (databases, artificial intelligence, machine learning, etc) that gives tools to discover structures, "interesting" knowledge and patterns in large data sets. It is also defined as the set of algorithms and methods for the exploration and analysis of (often) large computer databases to detect in the data: rules, associations, unknown trends ... that can enhance decision systems (I.H. Witten and al., 2011). The knowledge extraction process from data that commonly uses data mining algorithms is a succession of three main steps: data pre-processing, pattern recognition and interpreting results.

Data mining tools can be used within CEHL to extract knowledge from learning sessions' databases. This knowledge will be used to give an adaptive guidance for the learner so that he/she improve her/his progression. Three application areas have received special attention in the field of educational data mining:

- To improve the learner's model and provide detailed information about his/her characteristics such as knowledge, motivation or attitudes.
- To use the data mining process in modelling individual differences among learners (Baker et al., 2008).
- To discover or to improve, in their areas of application, the models concerning the structure of contents or the taught domains such as in (Shih, B., Koedinger, K.R., Scheines, R., 2008).
- To study educational support provided by the CEHL systems by studying how each type of instructional support can improve learning. Among the works on this problem, we have (Beck, J.E., Mostow, J., 2008).

We found too few research works on knowledge extraction from an automated and formative evaluation based on errors detection in learning by doing mode. In this paper, we focus on improving learner's model based on knowledge extraction process, using data mining algorithms and data from formative evaluation results' according to ODALA approach.

The ODALA (Ontology Driven Auto-evaluation for Learning Approach) evaluation approach (Bouarab-Dahmani F., 2010) proposes a methodology and techniques for the development of an evaluation system based on the teaching domain or discipline ontology Onto-TDM. It is based on the learners' potential errors classified into different types (semantic, lexico-syntactic ...) in the case of learning by doing. The content to teach, that we call teaching domain, is represented by domain ontology where the main concepts are: notions composed of sub-notions and knowledge items, evaluation units, errors, examples. The ODALA process (Bouarab-Dahmani F., 2010) (Bouarab-Dahmani F. et al., 2011) contains: form analysis of learner's solutions, semantic analysis, marking process and learner's model update. After different ODALA cycles, we get in the learning system, a set of data about the learner's learning and behavior such as: committed errors, comprehensive indicators, exercises resolution matrix …

We discuss, in this chapter, a learning cycle with feedback loop incorporating formative assessment followed by application of data mining algorithms after each training session (see Figure 1). The resulted knowledge from the knowledge extraction process is injected, in an appropriate format, into the module that handles the management and monitoring of the learner to facilitate appropriate decisions.

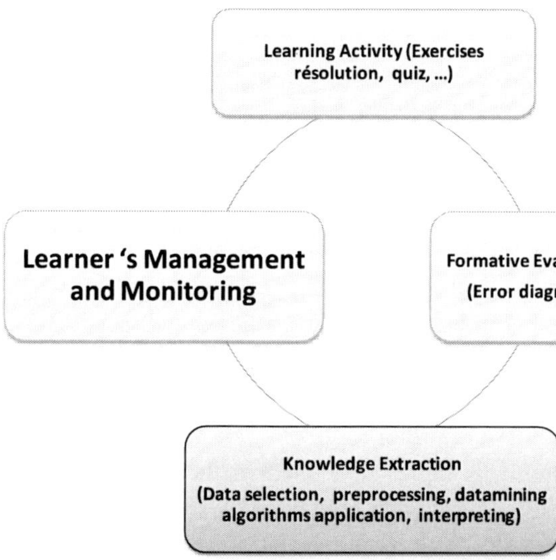

Figure 1. Learning Cycle integrating formative evaluation and knowledge extraction.

Currently, our interest concerns mainly the learner's management and monitoring and/or scaffolding going from formative evaluation results by:

- Recommendation of adequate learning content (courses, exercises ...)
- Identification of learning and performance differentiation between different groups of learners
- Discovery of frequents and/or relationships between errors and exercises, errors and learner profiles, ...
- Obstacles detection

For that, we are studying already existing algorithms and data mining tools in order to see their possible use for the exploration of formative evaluation data results based on ODALA approach. We conducted a set of tests, where the data got from the evaluation process of Websiela system was analyzed using mainly data mining algorithms implemented by the Weka tool (Ian, H. W., Eibe, F., 1999).

Weka (as java library or as a tool) is an open source device, developed at the University of Waikato in New Zealand. Websiela (Bouarab-Dahmani F., 2010) is a self-learning prototype for algorithmic based on ODALA approach. The next section gives an illustration of these tests with a limited set of data to make visible the results of the application of the C4.5 algorithms for classification, A *Priori* one for association rules discovery and K-means for clustering.

3. Mining Learning Data Using the Weka Tool

In addition to the ontological model of the domain to teach, data about the learner (from the learner's model) and the applied pedagogy (scenarios, parameters, … from the pedagogy model), we made recourse to other structures about the learning sessions where data about the learning activities (such as the exercises done, the detected errors, the pages visited, ...) are stored. This data is the most important to analyze. It expresses semantic rules, represented in the database as tables and used in the tests described in this paper to extract knowledge. For example we have these rules:

- A student can be enrolled in one or more sessions,
- each exercise can have more than one solution,
- an exercise can evaluate different knowledge items,
- an error refers to one knowledge item,
- a learner can perform different errors in a session when solving an exercise.

The relational tables considered in the tests are given in Table 1 with only the attributes used in the experiments.

The approach followed for each test, where data is analyzed by a data mining algorithm implemented in Weka tool, is composed of these steps:

- Setting of a goal
- Selection of the relational tables involved

- Pre-processing of the selected tables by algebraic calculation (application of relational algebraic operators such as: selection, natural join …) and translation to the adequate data format (the *.arff* format in the case of input data for algorithms implemented in Weka).
- Choice of the appropriate algorithm
- Execution of the algorithm from the tool Weka and/or from a JAVA application using the Weka API
- Analysis and interpretation of the results.

Table 1. Extract from the relational diagram of a CEHL database

Relationship	Commentary
- **Learner** (Id_learner, Name, E-mail, level)	Belongs to the learner's model
- **Session** (session_id, start_date, end_date, *id_learner)*	Session of a learner
)	exercises table
-**Error** (id_error, label_error, type_error, *id_ic)*	Table of potential errors. *Id_ic* is the identifier of the knowledge item, a granular component of the domain, to which it corresponds Table of Knowledge items, the granular components of the field to teach
-(session_id, id_error, id_exercise, Nb-occ)	Table of the errors committed by a given learner at a given session when solving a given exercise.
-**Evaluates** (id_exercise, id_ic, importance-degree)	Association between knowledge items and exercises with indication of the degree of importance of the knowledge item for the exercise

We tested different algorithms on different input data and for different objectives. The C4.5 algorithms for classification, K-Means for clustering and A Priori one for association rules discovery have attracted our attention during the various trials, for readability and relevance of their results. We report, in the following points of this paper some comments about the tests related to each of these three algorithms.

3.1. Classification of Learners with J 48 Algorithm

Classifiers are one of the commonly used tools in data mining. They take as input a collection of cases, each belonging to one of a small number of classes and described by its values for a fixed set of attributes, and output a classifier that can accurately predict the class to which a new case belongs (Wu et al., 2008).

The C4.5 algorithm (Quinlan, J.R., 1993) is one of the most cited algorithms for classification. It is an extension of the ID3 algorithm proposed by Quinlan for decision tree construction. One of the most attractive of decision trees aspects lies in the interpretation and construction of decision rules. The confidence of the rule is the proportion of records in the leaf node to which the decision rule is true. If confidence is 100% (= 1), the leaf node is pure and the decision rule is perfect.

We use the J48 algorithm which is an implementation of the C4.5 with the data collected during the execution of the WebSiela system, a prototype we developed for algorithmic learning with an automated correction of solutions freely built by learners to open questions. The input data table for the data mining process is deduced from a combination of the relational tables given in Table 1. We chose a very simple example concerning the classification of students according to the level that can be good, average or bad. This classification will clarify the relationship between a class (a level) and the number of errors (deduced from the input data).

To test the reliability and usability of the algorithm, we conducted disturbances in the input data to observe the reactions of the algorithm. In most cases, the results generated were adequate to the inputs. For example,

- At the test1, a learner is misclassified; he is ranked within good level when he has a number of errors equal to 12. This is shown in the decision tree result sheet bad decisions (3.0/1.0) as seen in Figure 2. So the algorithm can detect anomalies in our classification. For this case, we find the choice of two levels (3 and 4) perfectly adequate for the input data.
- For test 2, there are no misclassifications. We just added occurrences that might change the classes' thresholds (number of errors). As result, shown by Figure 3 and figure 4, the threshold for the "bad" class increased to 10.
- Test 3 showed a case of misclassification with the replacement of errors number for learners. The algorithm had evolved with the data

(see Figure 5), gave new adequate thresholds and detected the misclassification.

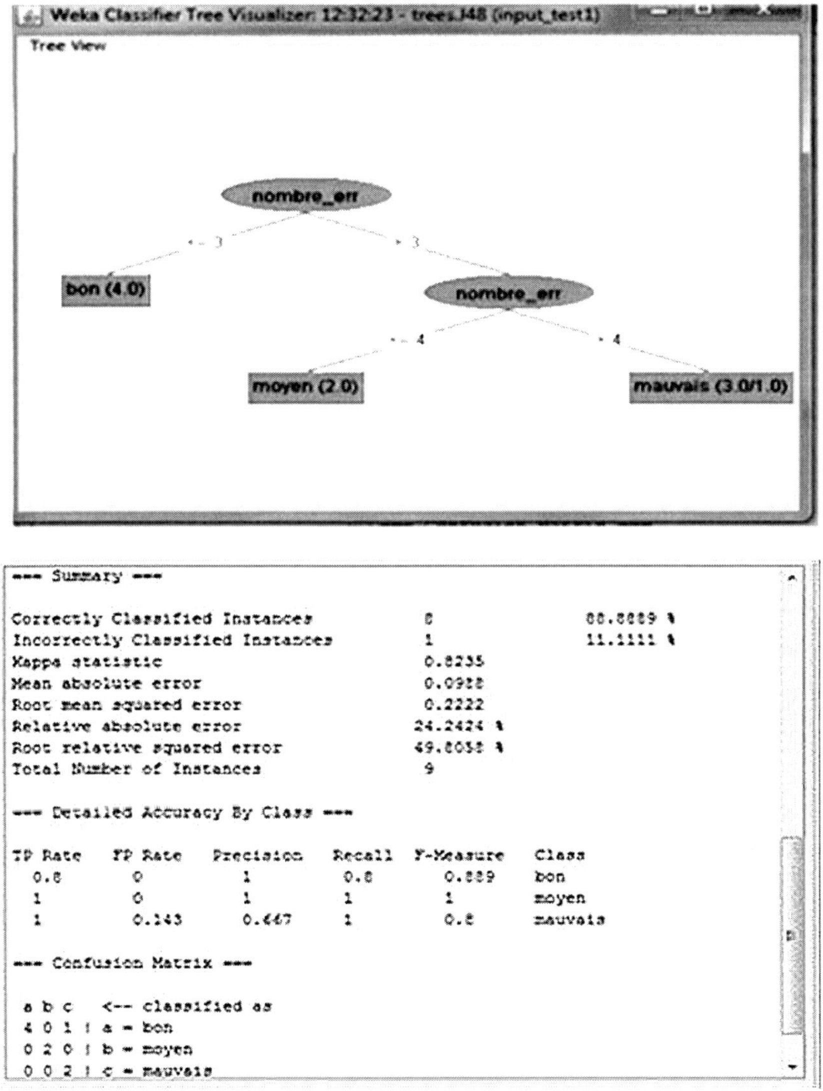

Figure 2. The result displayed in test 1.

```
=== Summary ===

Correctly Classified Instances          12              100      %
Incorrectly Classified Instances         0                0      %
Kappa statistic                          1
Mean absolute error                      0
Root mean squared error                  0
Relative absolute error                  0      %
Root relative squared error              0      %
Total Number of Instances               12

=== Detailed Accuracy By Class ===

TP Rate   FP Rate   Precision   Recall  F-Measure   Class
  1         0         1          1         1        bon
  1         0         1          1         1        mauvais
  1         0         1          1         1        moyen

=== Confusion Matrix ===

 a b c   <-- classified as
 5 0 0 | a = bon
 0 3 0 | b = mauvais
 0 0 4 | c = moyen
```

Figure 3. The textual result of test 2.

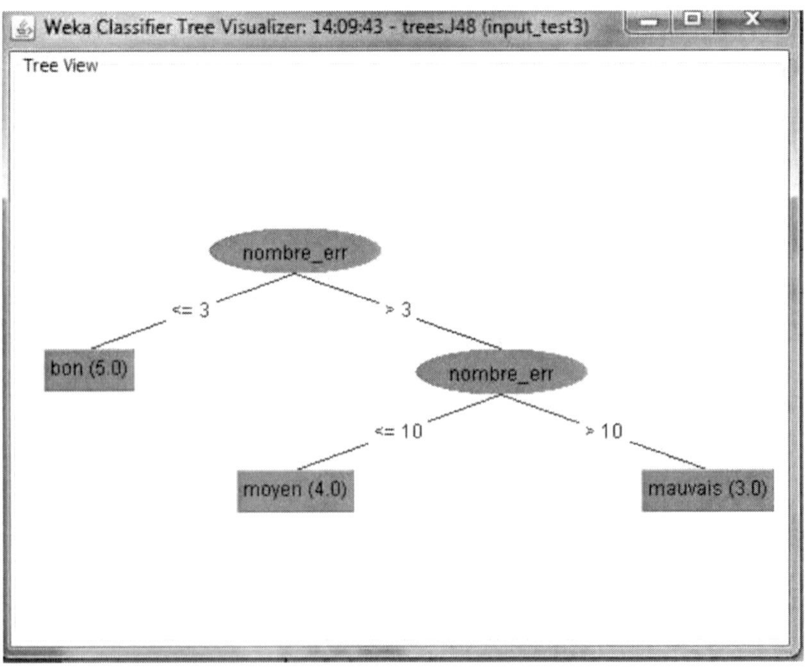

Figure 4. The graph of the classification (test 2).

```
=== Summary ===

Correctly Classified Instances          10               90.9091 %
Incorrectly Classified Instances         1                9.0909 %
Kappa statistic                          0.8625
Mean absolute error                      0.0909
Root mean squared error                  0.2132
Relative absolute error                 21      %
Root relative squared error             45.9573 %
Total Number of Instances               11

=== Detailed Accuracy By Class ===

TP Rate   FP Rate   Precision   Recall  F-Measure   Class
  0.8       0         1          0.8      0.889     bon
  1         0.125     0.75       1        0.857     mauvais
  1         0         1          1        1         moyen

=== Confusion Matrix ===

 a b c   <-- classified as
 4 1 0 | a = bon
 0 3 0 | b = mauvais
 0 0 3 | c = moyen
```

Figure 5. The textual result of test 3.

According to the different results of our tests on different input data, we deduced that the C4.5 algorithm is an interesting one for predictive classification of learners based on errors. The algorithm is flexible enough (one can change the criteria and select different attributes) so that it could suit different objectives.

3.2. Discovery of frequents with *A Priori* algorithm

A Priori algorithm (Agrawal R., Srikant R., 1994) is based on the fact that all common elements have subsets of common elements together. Indeed, if the set {A, B} is frequent in the database, the sets {A} and {B} are themselves frequent in the database. This algorithm generates rules involving correlated data. We have just to point out the set of attributes concerned by the analysis.

The objective chosen in this case was to look for correlations between the exercises, learners and errors detected in a learning session. The data to be included in the input table of the A Priori algorithm, called input_base2 (see Figure 6) is obtained by algebraic calculus on the two tables: Session, com-Error. We ran the algorithm directly on the three attributes: id-learner, id_exercise and id_error to extract all possible rules (the rule is given as if ... then form)

Viewer

Relation: apriori

No.	id_apprenant Nominal	id_exercice Nominal	id_erreur Nominal
1	1	1	1
2	1	1	2
3	1	2	4
4	1	3	0
5	3	2	3
6	3	2	3
7	3	2	4
8	3	3	0
9	2	1	1
10	2	1	2
11	2	3	0
12	4	2	4
13	4	3	0

Figure 6. The pre-processed input table 2.

Fichier input/ Test 1	**Results given by A Priori Algorithm with Weka/ Test 1**
@relation imput_test1 @attribute id_apprenant {1, 3, 2,4} @attribute id_exercice {1 ,2 ,3} @attribute id_erreur {1, 2, 4, NULL, 3} @data 1, 1, 1 1, 1, 2 1, 2, 4 1, 3, NULL 3, 2, 3 3, 2, 3 3, 2, 4 3, 3, NULL 2, 1, 1 2, 1, 2 2, 3, NULL 4, 2, 4 4, 3, NULL	Best rules found: 1. id_exercice=3 4 ==> id_erreur=NULL 4 conf:(1) 2. id_erreur=NULL 4 ==> id_exercice=3 4 conf:(1) 3. id_erreur=4 3 ==> id_exercice=2 3 conf:(1) 4. id_erreur=3 2 ==> id_apprenant=3 id_exercice=2 2 conf:(1) 5. id_apprenant=3 id_erreur=3 2 ==> id_exercice=2 2 conf:(1) 6. id_exercice=2 id_erreur=3 2 ==> id_apprenant=3 2 conf:(1) 7. id_erreur=3 2 ==> id_exercice=2 2 conf:(1) 8. id_erreur=2 2 ==> id_exercice=1 2 conf:(1) 9. id_erreur=1 2 ==> id_exercice=1 2 conf:(1) 10. id_erreur=3 2 ==> id_apprenant=3 2 conf:(1)

Figure 7. A result of A Priori execution under the tool Weka (test1).

Also, we put on different disturbances in the input data, for example: At the test1, we got a rule (Rule 1 in the screenshot of Figure 7) that we interpreted as: "regardless of the learner, the resolution of exercises 3 and 4 gave no error". The change in some instances of the input table gave a significant change in the generated rules. For example, we no longer had the rule 1 of test1 about exercises 3 and 4 (see Figure 8).

Fichier input/ Test 1	**Results given by A Priori Algorith with Weka/ Test 1**
Test 2	**Results given by A Priori Algorith with Weka/ Test 2**
relation imput_test2 @attribute id_apprenant {1, 3, 2, 4} @attribute id_exercice {1, 2, 3} @attribute id_erreur {1, 2, 4, NULL, 3,5} @data 1, 1, 3 1, 1, 5 1, 2, 4 **1, 3, 1** 3, 2, 3 3, 2, 4 3, 3, NULL 2, 1, 1 4, 3, NULL2, 1, 2 2, 3, NULL 4, 2, 4	Best rules found: 1. id_erreur=NULL 3 ==> id_exercice=3 3 conf:(1) 2. id_erreur=4 3 ==> id_exercice=2 3 conf:(1) 3. id_apprenant=3 id_erreur=3 2 ==> id_exercice=2 2 conf:(1) 4. id_exercice=2 id_erreur=3 2 ==> id_apprenant=3 2 conf:(1) 5. id_apprenant=4 id_exercice=3 1 ==> id_erreur=NULL 1 conf:(1) 6. id_apprenant=4 id_erreur=NULL 1 ==> id_exercice=3 1 conf:(1) 7. id_apprenant=4 id_exercice=2 1 ==> id_erreur=4 1 conf:(1) 8. id_apprenant=4 id_erreur=4 1 ==> id_exercice=2 1 conf:(1) 9. id_apprenant=2 id_exercice=3 1 ==> id_erreur=NULL 1 conf:(1) 10. id_apprenant=2 id_erreur=NULL 1 ==> id_exercice=3 1 conf:(1)

Figure 8. A result of A Priori execution under the tool Weka (Test 2).

After different tests, we deduced that the use of this algorithm could be of great help to enrich the formative evaluation or to get a global evaluation from the CEHL. However an automated interpretation of the derived rules will not be a simple task to develop and a "manual" interpretation will be very time consuming since all the generated rules are not systematically significant.

3.3. Learners Clustering with K-Means Algorithm

The k-means algorithm is a simple iterative method to partition a given dataset into a user-specified number of clusters, k (Wu et al., 2008). This algorithm has been discovered by several researchers across different disciplines, most notably Lloyd (1957, 1982), Forgey (1965), Friedman and Rubin (1967), and McQueen (1967). The cost of the optimal solution decreases with increasing k till it hits zero when the number of clusters equals the number of distinct data-points. K-means remains the most widely used algorithm for clustering in practice (Wu et al., 2008).

Relation: table1

No.	1: Id_app Numeric	2: nombre_err Numeric	3: nombre_exo Numeric
1	1.0	1.0	1.0
2	2.0	2.0	1.0
3	3.0	1.0	1.0
4	4.0	13.0	3.0
5	5.0	0.0	1.0
6	6.0	0.0	1.0
7	7.0	1.0	2.0
8	8.0	0.0	1.0
9	9.0	6.0	2.0
10	10.0	11.0	3.0
11	11.0	12.0	3.0
12	12.0	11.0	2.0
13	13.0	6.0	2.0
14	14.0	3.0	1.0
15	15.0	2.0	1.0
16	16.0	9.0	2.0
17	17.0	6.0	2.0
18	18.0	8.0	2.0
19	19.0	10.0	3.0
20	20.0	12.0	3.0
21	21.0	11.0	2.0
22	22.0	10.0	2.0
23	23.0	15.0	3.0
24	24.0	0.0	1.0
25	25.0	3.0	1.0
26	26.0	4.0	1.0
27	27.0	4.0	1.0
28	28.0	5.0	1.0
29	29.0	6.0	2.0
30	30.0	10.0	2.0

Figure 9. The input table of clustering tests.

We used K-means implemented in Weka on different datasets deduced from our educational database. In what follows, we propose an example (see Figure 9) where we have a view on each learner with the number of exercises done and the number of committed errors. The input table has just thirty (30) entries so that we can easily follow and analyze the results. The data mining objective in the case of this test is to get clusters of learners going with the number of their errors and/or number of exercises done.

Figure 10 shows the execution results of K-means via Weka with the number of clusters K=2. We can easily interpret the results given where:

Full data: is the general average of all the instances of each attribute.

Cluster 0 (first cluster found) has 9,75 as average of error numbers and 2,375 average for exercises numbers done. This cluster has Sixteen (16) learners.

Cluster 1 (the second cluster found) contains fourteen (14) learners with the average of 2,0714 for the errors numbers and 1,0714 for the average of exercises numbers done.

```
=== Run information ===
Scheme: weka.clusterers.SimpleKMeans -N 2 -A "weka.core.EuclideanDistance -R first-last" -I 500 -S 10
Relation: table1
Instances: 30
Attributes: 3
 nombre_err
 nombre_exo
Ignored:
 id_app
Test mode: evaluate on training data
=== Clustering model (full training set) ===
kMeans
======
Number of iterations: 2
Within cluster sum of squared errors: 2.2169753086419752
Missing values globally replaced with mean/mode
Cluster centroids:
 Cluster#
Attribute Full Data 0 1
 (30) (12) (18)
==============================================
nombre_err 6.1667 11 2.9444
nombre_exo 1.7667 2.5 1.2778
Time taken to build model (full training data) : 0.02 seconds
=== Model and evaluation on training set ===
Clustered Instances
0 12 ( 40%)
1 18 ( 60%)
```

Figure 10. Screen result of clustering with the tool Weka (test1).

The interpretation can be: The algorithm divided the learners on two clusters: those with one (1) exercise done with number of errors between 0 and 5 and those who did 2 or 3 exercises and the number of errors found is between 6 and 15. Figure 11 shows a clustering with K= 3 and on two attributes: the number of exercises done and the errors number. We can see then that the characteristics of the clusters found have changed.

```
=== Run information ===
Scheme: weka.clusterers.SimpleKMeans -N 3 -A "weka.core.EuclideanDistance
 -R first-last" -I 500 -S 10
Relation: table1
Instances: 30
Attributes: 3
 nombre_err
 nombre_exo
Ignored: id_app
Test mode: evaluate on training data
=== Clustering model (full training set) ===
kMeans
======
Number of iterations: 3
Within cluster sum of squared errors: 0.49184667184667175
Missing values globally replaced with mean/mode
Cluster centroids:
 Cluster#
Attribute Full Data 0 1 2
 (30) (6) (13) (11)
=====================================================
nombre_err 6.1667 12.1667 1.9231 7.9091
nombre_exo 1.7667 3 1 2
Time taken to build model (full training data): 0 seconds
=== Model and evaluation on training set ===
Clustered Instances
0 6 ( 20%)
1 13 ( 43%)
2 11 ( 37%)
```

Figure 11. Screen result of clustering with the tool Weka (test2).

```
=== Run information ===
Scheme: weka.clusterers.SimpleKMeans -N 2 -A "weka.core.EuclideanDistance -R first-last" -I 500 -S 10
Relation: table1
Instances: 30
Attributes: 3
 nombre_exo
Ignored:
 id_app
 nombre_err
Test mode: evaluate on training data
=== Clustering model (full training set) ===
kMeans
======
Number of iterations: 2
Within cluster sum of squared errors: 0.9705882352941179
Missing values globally replaced with mean/mode
Cluster centroids:
 Cluster#
Attribute Full Data 0 1
 (30) (17) (13)
==========================================
nombre_exo 1.7667 2.3529 1
Time taken to build model (full training data) : 0 seconds
=== Model and evaluation on training set ===
Clustered Instances
0 17 ( 57%)
1 13 ( 43%)
```

Figure 12. Screen result of clustering with the tool Weka (test3).

Figure 12 shows clustering on only the number of exercises done (the other attributes of the input table are "ignored").

We note then that the characteristics of the clusters found have changed compared to those of Figure 10.

4. DATA MINING IMPLEMENTATION IN A CEHL

We have deduced, after the tests described above, the interest of some data mining algorithms for formative evaluation results' analysis such as the C4.5, K-Means and the A Priori algorithms. The question, after that, is "How to integrate such algorithms in a CEHL?"

We have studied this problematic for the case of WebSiela system and the Weka API. We have developed two alternatives: The first one is a simple access interface to Weka tool from WebSiela with recovery of results. In this case, the interpreting step will be done by a human expert. The second alternative is related to the development of a module for an automated knowledge extraction process calling data mining algorithms with possible integration of an automated pre processing and interpreting (see Figure 13 to see the developed prototype interface).

Figure 13. Interface of the WebSiela data mining with Weka algorithms.

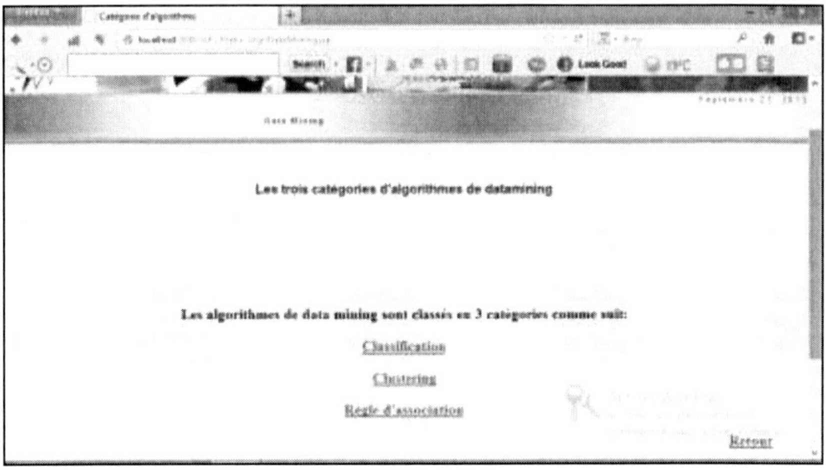

Figure 14. The links to the data mining tasks.

At this level of our work, we have implemented the preprocessing and knowledge extraction using the Weka API. The preprocessing module gives the needed .arff file automatically going from a relational database using adequate requests and attributes selection. The data mining of the obtained file is got by the execution of the Weka API algorithms. We tested the three algorithms cited above: A priori, J-48 and the K-Means (each for a specific task as seen in the interface of Figure 14).

In both cases, when we use without improvements and changes the algorithms implemented in Weka, the generated results can't be integrated and effectively used in the learning loop given in Figure 1. Consequently, this leads to specific programs creation particularly for the algorithms' results interpreting and even for preprocessing since the input data can have initially different format (XML, OWL, text …). For the case of frequents detection, we think that we need an improvement of the A priori algorithm or another way for associative rules detection.

This is in one side of our study. In an another side, the result of our experiments, shows the interest of the information that could automatically be generated from data mining for global formative evaluation, personalization, recommendation ... and other activities for the learners' management and monitoring, particularly important in the case of competency based approach. The Weka system can be used to test the interest and feasibility of an algorithm before programming it in a specific use for educational data mining or for a given use case. In addition, clustering and classification need just a simple interpreting program.

CONCLUSION

We explored, in this chapter, the use and integration of the Weka algorithms for educational data mining within a CEHL adopting learning by doing in the context of competency-based approach. This exploration was done by the execution of some algorithms implemented in the Weka tool first on a limited set of data and after that with data collected in the WebSiela system. The use of these algorithms was to explore the results of a formative evaluation based on ODALA approach. The observed results, especially through the execution of predictive classification with the C4.5 algorithm, the associative rules detection with A Priori algorithm and K-means algorithm for clustering, are interesting to track learner's progress. However, the A priori algorithm as implemented in Weka gives results difficult to interpret automatically and even by human in the case of big data. Finally to realize the loop of the learning process with a knowledge extraction module, we need specific programs development that can use the Weka API in the implementation step for clustering and classification. For frequents detection, we have to study deeply the A priori algorithm and even other association rules detection algorithms to get interpretable results. We have also the research perspective concerning the development of an automated and reusable filter and interpreter of the algorithms results and complete the loop of the learning process where the data mining results are used to update the learners' models or e-portfolios.

REFERENCES

Agrawal R., Srikant R., 1994. "Fast Algorithms for Mining Association Rules in Large Databases" *Proc. of the 20th Int'l Conf. on Very Large Data Bases (VLDB).* June 1994, p. 478-499. IBM Research Report RJ 9839.

Baker, R.S.J.d., Corbett, A.T., Aleven, V. (2008) "More Accurate Student Modelling Through Contextual Estimation of Slip and Guess Probabilities in Bayesian Knowledge Tracing" *Proceedings of the 9th International Conference on Intelligent Tutoring Systems*, 406-415, 2008.

Beck, J.E., Mostow, J. (2008) "How who should practice: Using learning decomposition to evaluate the efficacy of different types of practice for different types of students" *Proceedings of the 9th International Conference on Intelligent Tutoring Systems*, 353-362.

Bouarab-Dahmani F. (2010). *Modélisation basée ontologies pour l'apprentissage interactif - Application à l'évaluation des connaissances de l'apprenant.* Doctorate thesis in computer science of Mouloud Mammeri University, Tizi Ouzou, Algeia, 2010.

Bouarab-Dahmani F., Si-Mohammed M., Comparot C., Charrel P. J. (2011) "Adaptive Exercises Generation using an Automated Evaluation and a Domain Ontology: The ODALA+ Approach", *International journal of emerging technologies in learning*, IJET, Vol.6, Issue 2, June 2011, 4-10.

Ian, H. W., Eibe, F. (1999). *Data Mining: Practical Machine Learning Tools and Techniques with Java Implementations.* Morgan Kaufmann, October 1999.

Quinlan, J.R. (1993). C4.5: *Programs for Machine Learning.* Morgan Kaufmann 1993.

Romero, C. and Ventura, S. (2007) "Educational data mining: A Survey from 1995 to 2005. *Expert Systems with Applications*", (33), pp. 135-146.

Shih, B., Koedinger, K.R., Scheines, R. (2008) "A Response-Time Model for Bottom-Out Hints as Worked Examples". *Proceedings of the First International Conference on Educational Data Mining*, 117-126, 2008.

Witten I.H., Eibe F., Hall M.A. (2011). *Data Mining, Practical Machine Learning Tools and Techniques.* Third edition published in January 2011 by Morgan Kaufmann Publishers (ISBN: 978-0-12-374856-0).

(Wu et al., 2008). X.Wu, V. Kumar, J. R. Quinlan, J. Ghosh, Q. Yang, H. Motoda, G. J. McLachlan, A. Ng, B. Liu, P. S. Yu,·Z.H. Zhou, M. Steinbach, D. J. Hand, D. Steinberg. *Top 10 algorithms in data mining. Knowl Inf Syst (2008) 14:1–37. DOI 10.1007/s10115-007-0114-2.*

In: Data Mining
Editor: Harold L. Capri
ISBN: 978-1-63463-738-1

Chapter 3

MODELING NATIONS' FAILURE VIA DATA MINING TECHNIQUES

Mohamed M. Mostafa, Ph.D.
Gulf University for Science and Technology, Kuwait

ABSTRACT

Since the concept of 'failed states' was coined in the early 1990s, it has come to occupy a top tier position in the international peace and security's agenda. This study uses data mining techniques to examine the effect of various social, economic and political factors on states' failure at the global level. Data mining techniques use a broad family of computationally intensive methods that include decision trees, neural networks, rule induction, machine learning and graphic visualization. Three artificial neural network models: multi-layer perceptron neural network (MLP), radial basis function neural network (RBFNN) and self-organizing maps neural network (SOM) and one machine learning technique (support vector machines [SVM]) are compared to a standard statistical method (linear discriminant analysis (LDA). The variable sets considered are demographic pressures, movement of refugees, group paranoia, human flight, regional economic development, economic decline, delegitimization of the state, public services' performance, human rights status, security apparatus, elites' behavior and the role played by other states or external political actors. The study shows how it is possible to identify various dimensions of states' failure by uncovering complex patterns in the dataset, and also shows the classification abilities of data mining techniques.

Keywords: Failed states, neural networks, machine learning, computational intelligence

1. Introduction and Literature Survey

Helman and Ratner (1993) defined failed states as those states that are simply unable to function as independent entities. Helman and Ratner's classification included nations such as Haiti, Yugoslavia, the USSR, Sudan, Liberia, and Cambodia. Zartman (1995) defined failed states as those in which "the basic functions of the state are no longer performed" (p. 2). Zartman's classification included nations such as Congo of the 1960s; Chad, Ghana and Uganda of the early 1980s; and Somalia, Liberia and Ethiopia of the early 1990s. Hehir (2007) argues that failed states suffer from both "coercive incapacity" represented by monopolizing the use of force by the state and "administrative incapacity" which involves a failure to provide the basic services that most citizens expect from modern governments, such as a certain level of personal security, economic stability, and functioning bureaucratic and judicial systems. Using a multinomial logit model, Howard (2008) found that the transition to a failing state is positively influenced by the presence of a strong autocratic regime, state corruption and economic insecurity. However, Lambach (2004) argues that there is no fine line between state failure and non-failure. The author rather distinguishes between weak states that may still be able to provide some level of political goods and collapsed states that cannot guarantee even a modicum of order.

The 9/11 attacks brought failed states to the top tier of international peace and security's agenda. Afghanistan's failure to combat Al-Qaeda has lent a new attention to the concept because failed states were seen as safe harbors and launching pads for terrorism and terrorist organizations. For example, in a recent empirical study, Piazza (2008) found that the Failed States Index is a significant predictor of transnational terrorism. Using a series of negative binomial regressions, the author also found that states plagued by chronic state failures are statistically more likely to host terrorist groups and are more likely to be targeted by transnational terrorists themselves.

Although the failed states concept has emerged as a testable concept almost 20 years ago, no previous studies have attempted to use computational intelligence techniques to predict, classify and cluster failed nations and nations with high political risk. In this research we aim to fill this research gap by predicting, classifying and clustering state failure across 177 nations through the use of intelligent modeling techniques. More specifically, the purpose of this research is twofold:

- To determine the major factors that affect the state failure at the global level; and
- To benchmark the performance of computational intelligence models against traditional statistical techniques.

Thus, this paper makes at least two important contributions to the broader literature on state failure. First, most previous studies devoted to understand the state failure phenomenon are comprised of case study evaluations of few failed states (e.g., Lemarchand, 2003; Reno, 2003). Our study includes 177 nations, which makes it the most comprehensive study so far. By doing so the study adds depth to the knowledge base on state failure. Second, by employing computational intelligence methods such as neural networks and support vector machines, the study adds breadth to the debate over the causes of state failure at the global level. The paper is organized as follows. The next section summarizes the methodology used to conduct the analysis. The subsequent section presents empirical results of the analysis. Next, the paper sets out some implications of the analysis. This section also deals with the research limitations and explores avenues for future research.

2. METHOD

2.1. Multi-Layer Perceptron

MLP consists of sensory units that make up the input layer, one or more hidden layers of processing units (perceptrons), and one output layer of processing units (perceptrons). The MLP performs a functional mapping from the input space to the output space. The output of an MLP is compared to a target output and an error is calculated. This error is back-propagated to the neural network and used to adjust the weights. This process aims at minimizing the mean square error between the network's prediction output and the target output.

One of the first successful applications of MLP is reported by Lapedes and Farber (1988). Using two deterministic chaotic time series generated by the logistic map and the Glass-Mackey equation, they designed an MLP that can accurately mimic and predict such dynamic nonlinear systems. There is an extensive literature in financial applications of MLP (e. g. Kumar and Bhattacharya, 2006; Harvey et al., 2000). Another major application of MLP is in electric load consumption (e.g., Darbellay and Slama, 2000; McMenamin and Monforte, 1998). Many other problems have been solved by MLP. A short list includes air pollution forecasting (e.g., Videnova et al., 2006), maritime traffic forecasting (Mostafa, 2009), airline passenger traffic forecasting (Nam and Yi., 1997), railway traffic forecasting (Zhuo et al., 2007), commodity prices (Kohzadi et al., 1996), ozone level (Ruiz-Suarez et at., 1995), student grade point averages (Gorr et al., 1994), forecasting macroeconomic data (Aminian et al., 2006), advertising (Poh et at., 1998), and market trends (Aiken and Bsat, 1999).

The MLP is the most frequently used neural network technique in pattern recognition (Bishop, 2006) and classification problems (Sharda, 1994). However, numerous researchers document the disadvantages of the MLP approach. For example, Calderon and Cheh (2002) argue that the standard MLP network is subject to problems of local minima. Swicegood and Clark (2001) claim that there is no formal method of deriving a MLP network configuration for a given classification task. Thus, there is no direct method of finding the ultimate structure for modeling process. Consequently, the refining process can be lengthy, accomplished by iterative testing of various architectural parameters and keeping only the most successful structures. Wang (1995) argues that standard MLP provides unpredictable solutions in terms of classifying statistical data.

2.2. Radial Basis Function Neural Network

The basic architecture for a RBFNN is a 3-layer network. The input layer is simply a fan-out layer and does no processing. The second or hidden layer performs a non-linear mapping from the input space into a higher dimensional space in which the patterns become linearly separable. The final layer therefore performs a simple weighted sum with a linear output.

The unique feature of the RBFNN is the process performed in the hidden layer. The idea is that the patterns in the input space form clusters. If the centers of these clusters are known, then the distance from the cluster centre can be measured. Furthermore, this distance measure is made non-linear, so that if a pattern is in an area that is close to a cluster centre it gives a value close to 1. Beyond this area, the value drops dramatically. The notion is that this area is radially symmetrical around the cluster centre, so that the non-linear function becomes known as the radial-basis function.

Since the RBFNN has only one hidden layer and has fast convergence speed, it is widely used for non-linear mappings between inputs and outputs. Examples include detecting spam email (Jiang, 2007), financial distress prediction (Cheng et al., 2006), public transportation (Celikoglu & Cigizoglu, 2007), classification of active components in traditional medicine (Liu et al., 2009), classification of audio signals (Dhanalakshmi et al., 2009), prediction of athletes performance (Iyer & Sharda, 2009), and face recognition (Balasubramanian et al., 2009).

2.3. Support Vector Machines

SVMs have been developed by Vapnik (1995) as a novel type of machine learning. SVMs are a set of related supervised learning methods used for classification and regression. In the case of classification, SVMs obtain the 'optimal' boundary of two classes in a vector space independently on the probabilistic distributions of training vectors in the data set. If the categories are linearly separated, the aim of SVMs is to find the 'optimal' hyperplane boundary which separates both classes, classifying not only the training set but also unknown samples. When the classes are non-linearly separable, the input data are implicitly mapped into a higher dimensional space by a kernel function, e.g., Guassian radial basis function (Berrueta et al., 2007).

SVMs are based on the structure risk minimization (SRM) principle, which has been shown to be superior to the traditional risk minimization (ERM) principle employed by neural networks (Kecman, 2005). SRM minimizes an upper bound of the generalization error on the Vapnik-Chernoverkis (VC) dimension, as opposed to ERM, which minimizes the training error. Recently, Li et al., (2008) found that SVMs have better modeling performance than the MLP in short-term freeway traffic volume forecasting. Compared to neural networks, other SVMs advantages include their strong theoretical basis which provides them with high generalization capability. SVMs always have a solution, which can be quickly obtained by a standard quadratic programming algorithm.

SVMs have been used in a range of areas like financial applications (e.g., Ravi et al., 2008), classification of fragrance properties (Luan et al., 2008), dynamic classification for video stream (Awad & Motai, 2008), classification of forest fire types (Koetz et al., 2008), consumer churn prediction

(Coussement and Van den Poel, 2008), text categorization (Hmeidi et al., 2008), spam classification (Yu & Xu, 2008) and estimating production levels (Chen & Wang, 2007).

2.4. Self-Organizing Maps

The SOM, also called Kohonen map, is a heuristic model for exploring and visualizing patterns in high dimensional datasets. It was first introduced to the neural networks community by Kohonen (1982). SOM can be viewed as a clustering technique that identifies clusters in a dataset without the rigid assumptions of linearity or normality of more traditional statistical techniques. Indeed, like *k*-means, it clusters data based on an unsupervised competitive algorithm where each cluster has a fixed coordinate in a topological map (Audrain-Pontevia, 2006). The SOM is trained based on an unsupervised training algorithm where no target output is provided and the network evolves until convergence. Based on the Gladyshev's theorem, it has been shown that SOM models have almost sure convergence (Lo & Bavarian, 1993).

The SOM consists of only two layers: the input layer which classifies data according to their similarity, and the output layer of radial neurons arranged in a two-dimensional map. Output neurons will self-organize to an ordered map and neurons with similar weights are placed together. They are connected to adjacent neurons by a neighborhood relation, dictating the topology of the map (Moreno et al., 2006). The number of neurons can vary from a few dozen to several thousand. Since the SOM compresses information while preserving the most important topological and metrical relationships of the primary data elements on the display, it can also be used for pattern classification (Silven et al., 2003).

Due to the unsupervised character of their learning algorithm and the excellent visualization ability, SOMs have been recently used in myriad classification and clustering tasks. Examples include classifying cognitive performance in schizophrenic patients and healthy individuals (Silver & Shmoish, 2008), mutual funds classification (Moreno et al., 2006), speech quality assessment (Mahdi, 2006), vehicle routing (Ghaziri & Osman, 2006), network intrusion detection (Zhong et al., 2007), anomalous behavior in communication networks (Frota et al., 2007), compounds pattern recognition (Yan, 2006), market segmentation (Kuo et al., 2002), clustering green consumer behavior (Mostafa, 2009) and classifying magnetic resonance brain images (Chaplot et al., 2006).

3. RESULTS

3.1. Preliminary Data Analysis

Failed states data in this study were taken from the Fund for Peace (FundForPeace.org) and Foreign Policy magazine (2009). The failed states index (FSI) rates 12 social, economic and political indicators, derived from open-source materials. These 12 indicators are: mounting demographic pressures, massive movement of refugees and internally displaced persons, legacy of vengeance-seeking group grievance, chronic and sustained human flight, uneven economic development along group lines, sharp or severe economic decline, criminalization or de-ligitimazation of the state, progressive deterioration of public services, widespread violation of human rights, security apparatus as "state within state"", rise of factionalized elites, and intervention of other states or external actors. The rank order of the states shown in Figure 1 is based on the total scores of the 12 indicators. For each indicator, the ratings are placed on a scale of 0 to 10, with 0 being the lowest intensity (most stable) and 10 being the highest intensity (least stable). The total score is the sum of the 12 indicators and is on a scale of 0-120. In the 2009 index there are 177 states, compared to only 146 in 2006 and 75 in 2005. Only recognized sovereign states based on the UN membership are included in the analysis. Thus, several territories such as Taiwan, Palestine and Kosovo are excluded from the index. In 2009 the FSI ranged from 18.3 in Norway to 114.7 in Somalia. Furthermore, the Fund for Peace places nations into four categories based on their scores. The most at-risk countries are placed in the "Alert" category. This group includes nations having indices between 91 and 120; the "Warning" category is reserved for countries scoring between 61 and 90; the "Monitoring" category includes nations with a score ranging from 31 to 60; and the "Sustainable" category includes nations scoring between 12 and 30. Figure 2 shows boxplots for all variables used in the analysis.

Since the FSI is supposed to measure states "failure" dimension, factor analysis was conducted to ascertain the unidimensionality of the index. Using a standard eigenvalue of 1.0 (Child, 1990) and an inspection of a scree plot (Figure 3), factor analysis yielded one factor. Total variance explained (79.06 percent) exceeds the 60 percent threshold commonly used in social sciences to establish satisfaction with the solution (Hair et al., 1998). We used the Kaiser-Mayer-Olkin (KMO) measure of sampling adequacy (Kaiser, 1970) to measure the adequacy of the sample for extraction of the three factors.

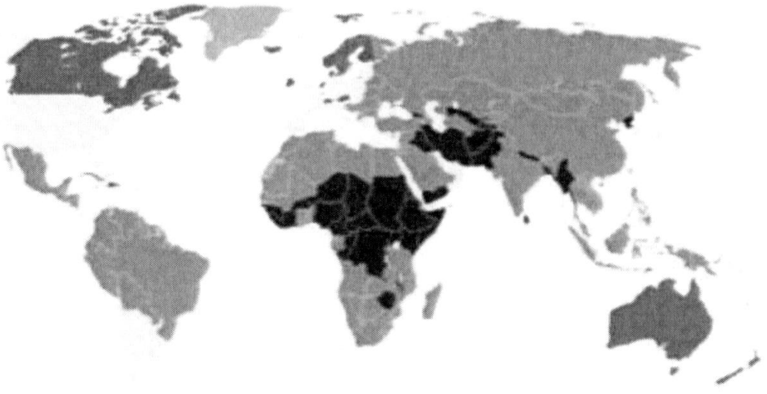

▌Alert Warning Monitoring/stable Sustainable/most stable No Information / Dependent Territory.

Figure 1. Failed States Index. Sources: The Fund for Peace (FundForPeace.org) and *Foreign Policy* (July/August, 2009, pp. 80-83).

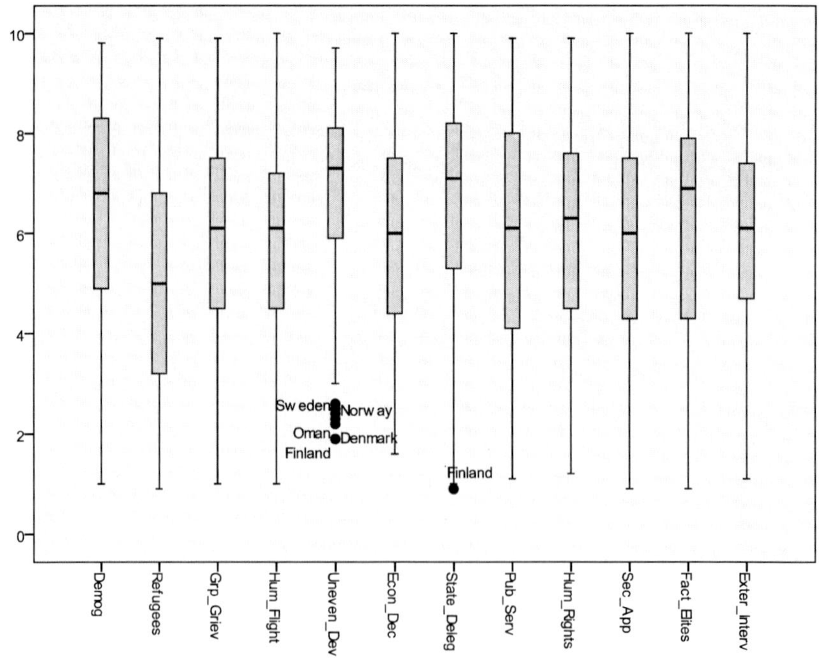

Figure 2. Boxplots of variables used in the analysis.

The KMO value found (0.942) is indicative of a data set considered to be highly desirable for factor analysis (Kim and Mueller, 1978). The Bartlett's test of sphericity, which tests whether the correlation matrix is an identity matrix, is significant (Approx. Chi-square=3055.735, df=66, p<0.001). This indicates the factor model is appropriate.

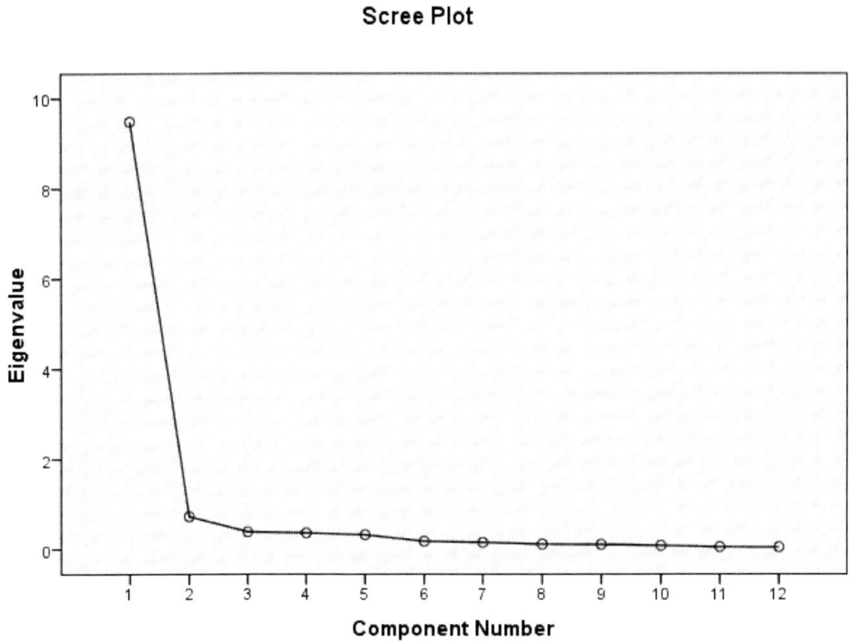

Figure 3. Scree plot of eigenvalues vs. components.

3.2. MLP, RBFNN and SVM-Based Classification

There are many software packages available for analyzing MLP models. We chose SPSS Neural Networks (SPSS, 2007) package. This software package applies artificial intelligence techniques to automatically find the efficient MLP architecture (MLP design used in this study is shown in Figure 4). Typically, the application of MLP requires a training data set and a testing data set (Lek and Guegan, 1999). The training data set is used to train the MLP and must have enough examples of data to be representative for the overall problem. The testing data set should be independent of the training set and is used to assess the classification accuracy of the MLP after training. Following Lim and Kirikoshi (2005), an error back-propagation algorithm with weight updates occurring after each epoch was used for MLP training. The learning rate was set at 0.1. Table 1 reports the properties of the MLP model. Table 2 shows the MLP classification accuracy. From table 2 we see that the MLP classifier predicted training sample with 97.2% accuracy and validation sample with 94.4% accuracy.

Figure 4. Multi-layer perceptron neural network architecture.

Table 1. MLP neural network configuration

Input Layer	Covariates	1	Demog
		2	Refugees
		3	Grp_Griev
		4	Hum_Flight
		5	Uneven_Dev
		6	Econ_Dec
		7	State_Deleg
		8	Pub_Serv
		9	Hum_Rights
		10	Sec_App
		11	Fact_Elites
		12	Exter_Interv
		Number of Units[a]	12
		Rescaling Method for Covariates	Standardized
Hidden Layer(s)		Number of Hidden Layers	1
		Number of Units in Hidden Layer 1[a]	5
		Activation Function	Hyperbolic tangent
Output Layer	Dependent Variables	1	Failed_Status
	Number of Units		4
	Activation Function		Softmax
	Error Function		Cross-entropy

a. Excluding the bias unit.

Table 2. MLP neural network classification

		Predicted				
Sample	Observed	bdrline	critical	in_dang	stable	Percent Correct
Training	bdrline	27	0	2	0	93.1%
	critical	0	34	0	0	100.0%
	in_dang	0	1	65	0	98.5%
	stable	1	0	0	11	91.7%
	Overall Percent	19.9%	24.8%	47.5%	7.8%	97.2%
Testing	bdrline	3	0	0	1	75.0%
	critical	0	4	0	0	100.0%
	in_dang	1	0	26	0	96.3%
	stable	0	0	0	1	100.0%
	Overall Percent	11.1%	11.1%	72.2%	5.6%	94.4%

Dependent Variable: Failed_Status.

RBFNN was also implemented using the SPSS Neural Networks (SPSS, 2007) package (RBFNN design used in this study is shown in Figure 5). The basic configuration of the RBFNN used is shown in Table 3. The learning rates for the RBFNN parameters are varied between 0.001 and 0.1 and that for the weights are varied between 0.1 and 0.7. The training is stopped if either the error goal reaches 0.001 or if the maximum misclassification becomes lower than one percent. Table 4 provides the basic RBFNN properties. From table 4 we see that the hit ratio for the training sample is 97.9% and the hit ratio for the validation sample is 97%.

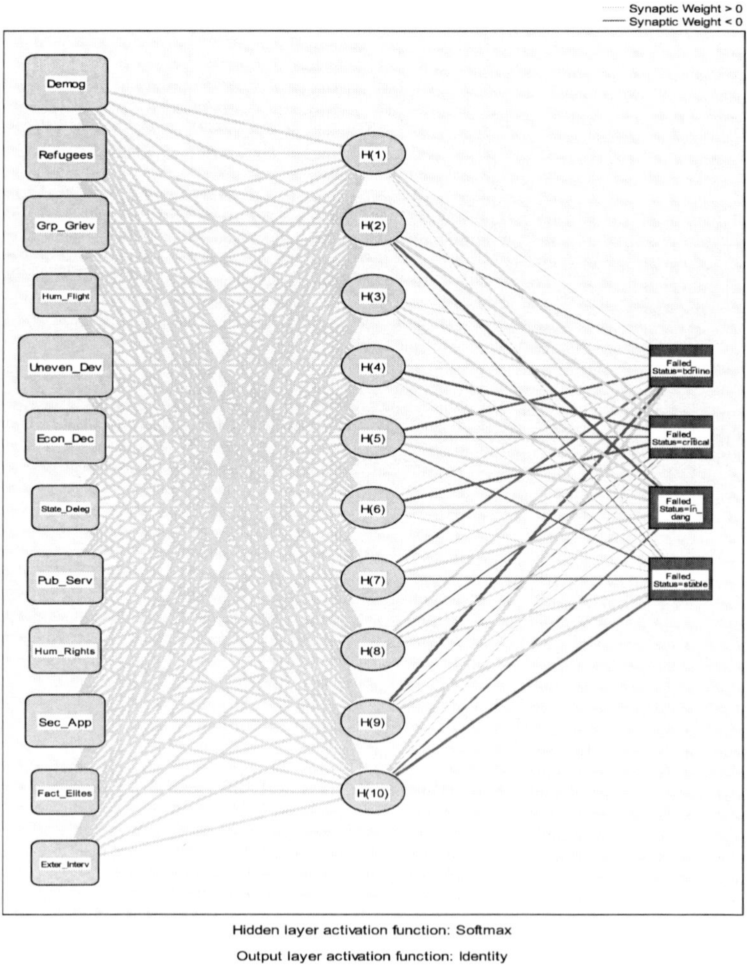

Figure 5. Radial basis function neural network architecture.

Table 3. RBF neural network configuration

Input Layer	Covariates	1	Demog
		2	Refugees
		3	Grp_Griev
		4	Hum_Flight
		5	Uneven_Dev
		6	Econ_Dec
		7	State_Deleg
		8	Pub_Serv
		9	Hum_Rights
		10	Sec_App
		11	Fact_Elites
		12	Exter_Interv
		Number of Units	12
		Rescaling Method for Covariates	Standardized
Hidden Layer		Number of Units	4[a]
		Activation Function	Softmax
Output Layer	Dependent Variables	1	Failed_Status
	Number of Units		4
	Activation Function		Identity
	Error Function		Sum of Squares

a. Determined by the testing data criterion: The "best" number of hidden units is the one that yields the smallest error in the testing data.

Table 4. RBF neural network classification

Sample	Observed	Predicted				
		bdrline	critical	in_dang	stable	Percent Correct
Training	bdrline	26	0	0	0	100.0%
	critical	0	28	1	0	96.6%
	in_dang	0	1	76	0	98.7%
	stable	1	0	0	11	91.7%
	Overall Percent	18.8%	20.1%	53.5%	7.6%	97.9%
Testing	bdrline	7	0	0	0	100.0%
	critical	0	9	0	0	100.0%
	in_dang	1	0	15	0	93.8%
	stable	0	0	0	1	100.0%
	Overall Percent	24.2%	27.3%	45.5%	3.0%	97.0%

Dependent Variable: Failed_Status.

SVMs were implemented using the SVM function in R software (Dimitradou et al., 2005). This function provides a user-friendly interface to the LIBSVM software developed by Chang and Lin (2001) along with visualization and parameter tuning methods. This function is currently one of the most widely used implementations of SVM algorithms as it provides a robust and fast SVM implementation and produces state of the art results on most classification and regression problems (Karatzoglou et al., 2005). Appendix A provides the R code used to conduct the SVM analysis. As seen in Figure 6, the correct classification rate for both training and test samples was 100%.

Figure 7 shows a contour plot of SVM performance at different levels of complexity.

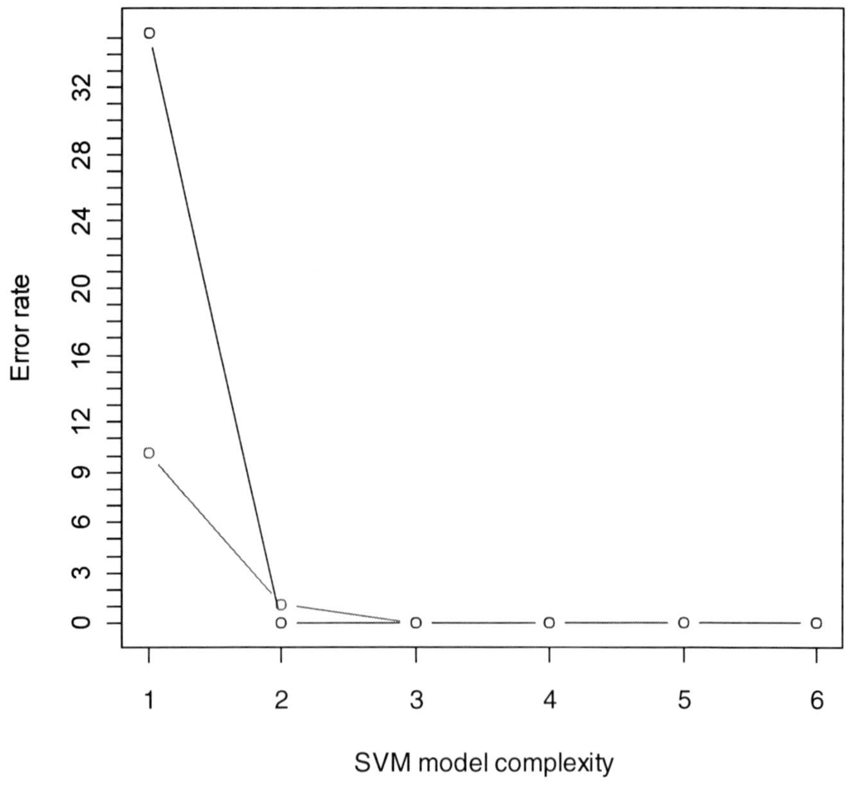

Figure 6. Support vector machine model complexity vs. error rate.

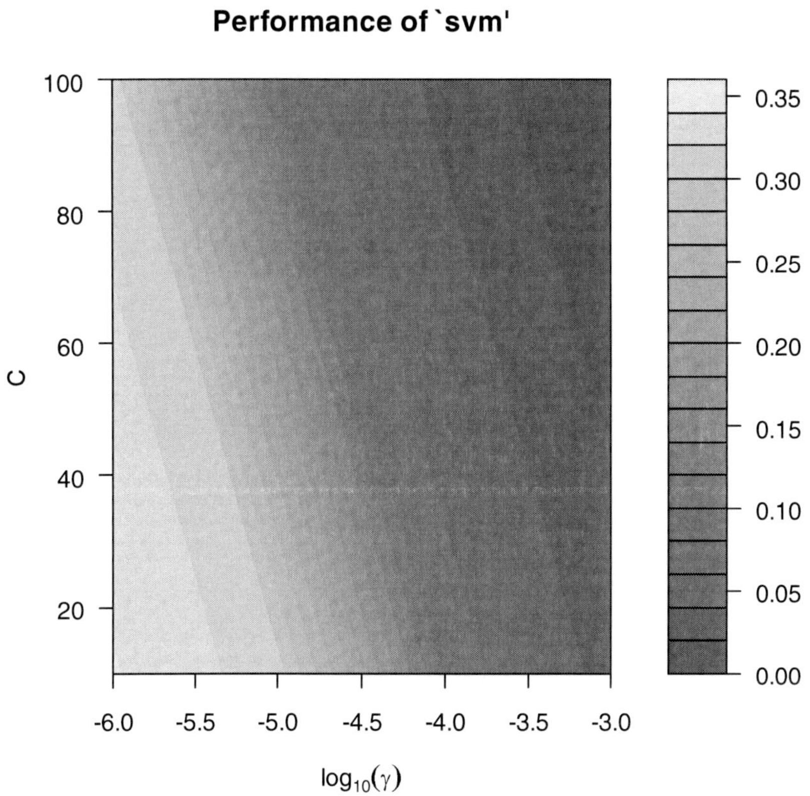

Figure 7. Contour plot of SVM performance.

To study the effectiveness of MLP, RBFNN and SVM-based classification of failed states, the results of MLP RBFNN and SVM were compared with the traditional multiple discriminant analysis (MDA). MDA is frequently used supervised pattern recognition technique. A linear function of the variables is sought, which maximizes the ratio of between-class variance and minimizes the ratio of within-class variance. MDA is an extremely simple and efficient method of classification. Indeed, it cannot be outperformed if the two distributions are normal and have the same dispersion matrix (i.e., Bayes limit). Figure 8 shows the canonical discriminant functions' failed states group centroids. A common measure of predictive models is the percentage of observation correctly classified or the hit ratio. The MDA model had an accuracy rate of 93.2%, with a leave-one-out validation accuracy of 86.4% as shown in Table 5.

Table 5. LDA classification results[b,c]

			Predicted Group Membership				
		Failed_Code	1.0	2.0	3.0	4.0	Total
Original	Count	1.0	38	0	0	0	38
		2.0	6	85	2	0	93
		3.0	0	1	29	3	33
		4.0	0	0	0	13	13
	%	1.0	100.0	.0	.0	.0	100.0
		2.0	6.5	91.4	2.2	.0	100.0
		3.0	.0	3.0	87.9	9.1	100.0
		4.0	.0	.0	.0	100.0	100.0
Cross-validated[a]	Count	1.0	38	0	0	0	38
		2.0	9	81	3	0	93
		3.0	0	3	22	8	33
		4.0	0	0	1	12	13
	%	1.0	100.0	.0	.0	.0	100.0
		2.0	9.7	87.1	3.2	.0	100.0
		3.0	.0	9.1	66.7	24.2	100.0
		4.0	.0	.0	7.7	92.3	100.0

a. Cross validation is done only for those cases in the analysis. In cross validation, each case is classified by the functions derived from all cases other than that case.

b. 93.2% of original grouped cases correctly classified.

c. 86.4% of cross-validated grouped cases correctly classified.

Figure 9 displays the MLP cumulative gain chart (similar figure was obtained for RBFNN). This chart shows the percentage of the overall number of cases in a given category gained by targeting a percentage of the total number of cases. For example, the first point on the curve for the in danger category is at (10%, 20%), meaning that if a dataset is scored with the network and all the cases are sorted by predicted pseudo-probability of donor, we would expect the top 10% to contain approximately 20% of all of the cases that actually take the category in danger. Likewise, the top 20% would contain approximately 40% of in danger states, and so on.

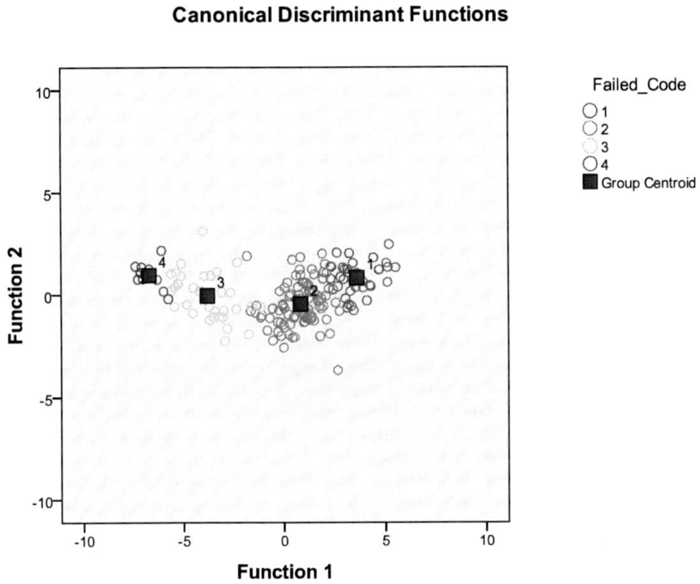

Figure 8. Failed states group centroids.

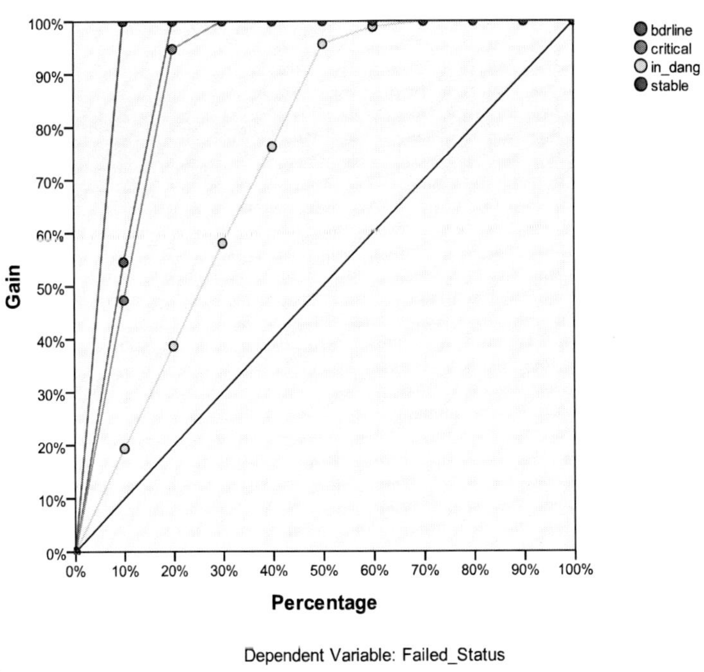

Figure 9. Multi-layer perceptron neural network gain chart.

The diagonal line is the baseline curve; if 10% of the cases are selected from the scored dataset at random, we would expect to gain approximately 10% of all of the cases that actually take the category donor. The farther above the baseline a curve lies, the greater the gain.

Despite the satisfactory classification performance of the MLP, RBFNN and SVM in this study, such models are often criticized as black boxes that do not allow decision-makers to make inferences on how the input variables affect the models' results. One way to address this issue is to conduct a variable impact analysis (VIA). The purpose of VIA is to measure the sensitivity of net predictions to changes in independent variables. Figure 10 shows that the most important input variables for the MLP are refugees, security apparatus and external intervention. Similar results were obtained using the RBFNN. The lower the percent value for a given variable, the less that variable affects the predictions. The results of the analysis can help in the selection of a new set of independent variables, one that will allow more accurate predictions. For example, a variable with a low impact value can be eliminated in favor of some new variables.

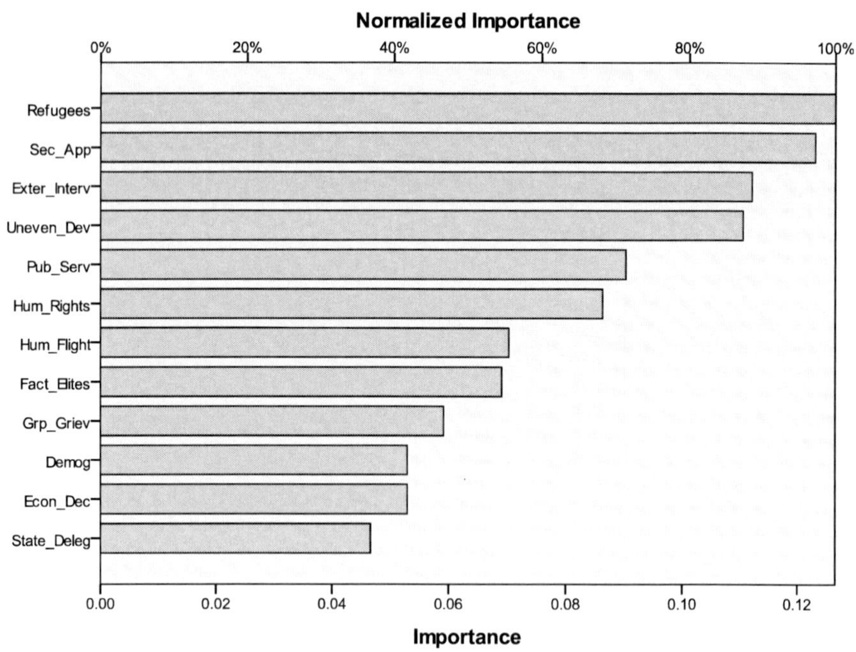

Figure 10. Multi-layer perceptron neural network variable impact analysis.

3.3. SOM-Based Clustering

There are many software packages available for analyzing SOM models. We chose SOMine package version 5.0 (Viscovery software, 2008). This software applies artificial intelligence techniques to automatically find the efficient SOM clusters. To visualize the cluster structure, some authors use the unified distance matrix (*U*-matrix) (e.g., Vijayakumar et al., 2007; Stavrou et al., 2010). However, this method does not give crisp boundaries to the clusters (Worner & Gevrey, 2006). In this study a hierarchical cluster analysis with a Ward linkage method was applied to the SOM to clearly delineate the edges of each cluster. The number of neurons is chosen to be 2000. There are two learning algorithms for SOM (Kohonen, 2001): the sequential or stochastic learning algorithm and the batch learning algorithm. In the former, the reference vectors are updated immediately after a single input vector is presented. In the latter, the update is done using all input vectors. While the batch algorithm does not suffer from convergence problems, the sequential algorithm is stochastic in nature and is less likely trapped to a local minimum. Following Ding & Patra (2007), we choose the sequential learning algorithm to train the SOM.

The SOM cluster results are shown in Figure 11. This two-dimensional hexagonal grid shows clear division of the input pattern into four clusters. Since the order on the grid reflects the neighborhood within the data, features of the data distribution can be read off from the emerging landscape on the grid. Figure 11 shows four discernable clusters of failed states. This four-cluster solution meets Siew et al., (2002) qualitative criteria that should be used to select the representative SOM model. These criteria include representability, explainability and level of sophistication. representability refers to the fact that the variables in each cluster should be distinct and carry some information of their own. This means that the resulting profile for each cluster should be unique and meaningful. Explainability means that the clusters themselves are distinct. Level of sophistication means that the size of each cluster should be monitored so that there are no either too large clusters that might hide more distinct groups in the cluster, or too small clusters that might be an indication of artificial clusters.

When assessing the quality of clustering model for validation purposes, quantitative criteria can also be used (Zhuang et al., 2009). We used the Kohonen software package (Wehrens and Buydens, 2007) to validate the cluster results.

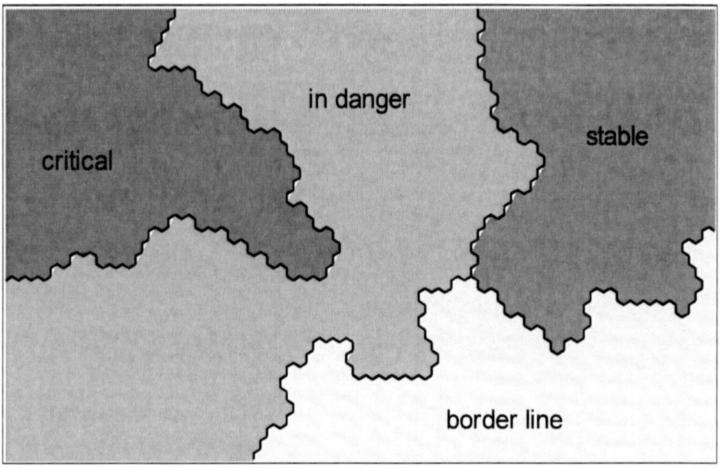

Figure 11. SOM-Ward clusters.

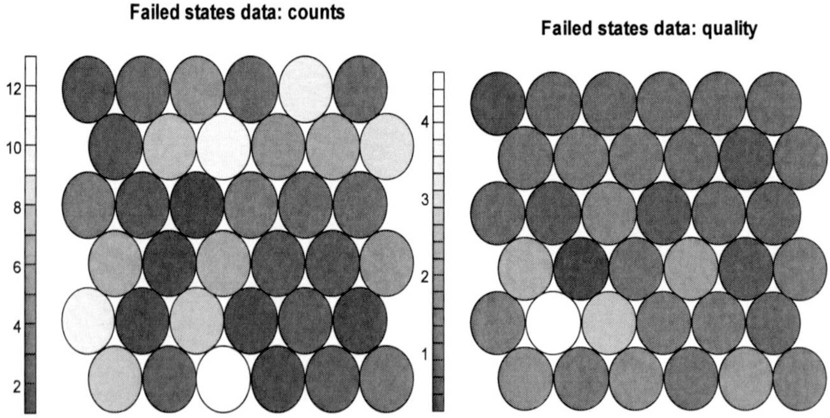

Figure 12. SOM counts and quality plots.

Figure 12 shows both the SOM counts and the mapping quality. In the left plot, the background color of a unit corresponds to the number of samples mapped to the unit. This figure shows that there is a reasonable spread out over the map. One of the units is empty (depicted in grey), which suggests that no samples have been mapped to it. The right plot shows the quality of the mapping. It represents the mean distance between objects mapped to a particular unit and the input vector of that unit. A good mapping should show small distances everywhere in the map. An alternative method, called the bi-directional Kohonen mapping (Melssen et al., 2006) has also been implemented. Results obtained are very similar to the ones obtained above. Another method to check the validity of the SOM during the training phase is to see whether the input vectors are becoming more and more similar to the closest objects in the dataset. Based on Figure 13 we see the effect of the neighborhood shrinking to include only the winning unit. This implies that there is no need for more iterations to optimize training parameters.

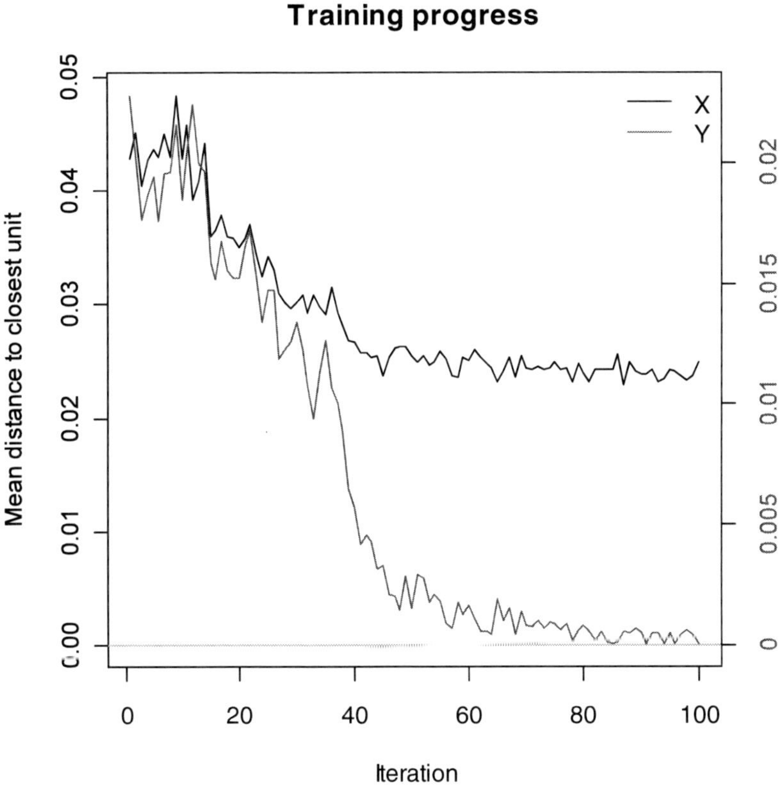

Figure 13. SOM neighborhood shrinkage plot.

Cluster 1 is called "critical." This is the green-colored cluster with a frequency of 21.47%. This cluster corresponds to the "alert." zone in the Fund for Peace classification. Cluster 2 is called "in danger." This blue-colored cluster has a frequency of 37.58%. This is the largest cluster and corresponds to the "warning" zone in the Fund for Peace classification. The third cluster is called "border line." This yellow-colored cluster has a frequency of 20.34%. This cluster corresponds to the "monitoring" zone in the Fund for Peace classification. Finally, the fourth cluster is labeled "stable." This cluster corresponds to the "sustainable" zone in the Fund for Peace classification Table 6 summarizes the basic information in each cluster. The SOM results validate the Fund for Peace and Foreign Policy classifications.

Based on the SOM-Ward clusters, feature or component maps can be constructed (Vesanto, 1999). These maps are also known in the literature as 'temperature maps.' (Churilov & Flitman, 2006). On these maps, the nodes which share similar information are organized in close color proximity to each other. Figure 14 shows the feature maps for every cluster and for all input attributes. Feature maps show the distribution of values of the respective input component over the map. Relationships between variables could be inspected by visually comparing the pattern of shaded pixels for each map; similarity of the patterns indicates strong monotonic relationships between the variables. The name of the displayed input component appears on top of each map. The color scale at the bottom of the component window shows that blue is used for low values, green for mid-range values and red for high values. From the feature maps we note, for example, that the "critical" cluster includes the highest constellation of red pixels for nations characterized by mounting demographic pressures, massive movement of refugees, group paranoia, chronic or sustained human flight, uneven economic development, sharp economic decline, delegitimization of the state, progressive deterioration of public services, widespread violation of human rights, strong security apparatus, factionalized elites and intervention of other states or external political actors. This implies that these variables are positively related to state failure- a result that was previously confirmed by other researchers (e.g., Howard, 2008). In essence, these colorful maps reveal the existence of previously theorized assumptions and it can even create new ones. The maps also make it possible to find subgroups that do not follow the main theoretical assumptions. For example, when red dots are found in the middle of the yellow or blue area, this signals the presence of deviant subgroups. When either blue or red nodes are forming two clearly separated areas, this might be considered as a sign of non-linear correlation (Thneberg & Hotulainen, 2006). Figure 15 shows the predictive ability of the SOM model for a randomly chosen set of the nations included in the analysis. For example, Zimbabwe is correctly classified as a critically failed nation, while Belgium is correctly classified as a stable nation (SOM prediction accuracy was 97.74%).

Table 6. SOM cluster summary

Seg.*	Freq %	Dem	Ref	Gr_Gr	Hu_Fl	Un_Dev	Ec_Dec	S_De	P_Ser	H_Ri	Sec_Ap	F_El	Ex_In
1	21.47	8.18	7.99	8.50	7.17	8.45	7.13	8.69	7.72	8.31	8.18	8.69	7.74
2	37.85	7.51	5.59	6.37	6.30	7.48	6.69	7.53	7.05	6.88	6.65	7.09	6.74
2	20.34	5.94	3.60	4.92	6.14	6.79	5.51	5.83	5.19	4.88	4.65	4.82	5.46
3	20.34	3.45	2.48	3.69	2.53	4.10	3.41	2.94	2.44	2.98	2.21	2.83	3.03

Seg*: 1= critical; 2 = in danger; 3 =borderline; and 4 = stable.

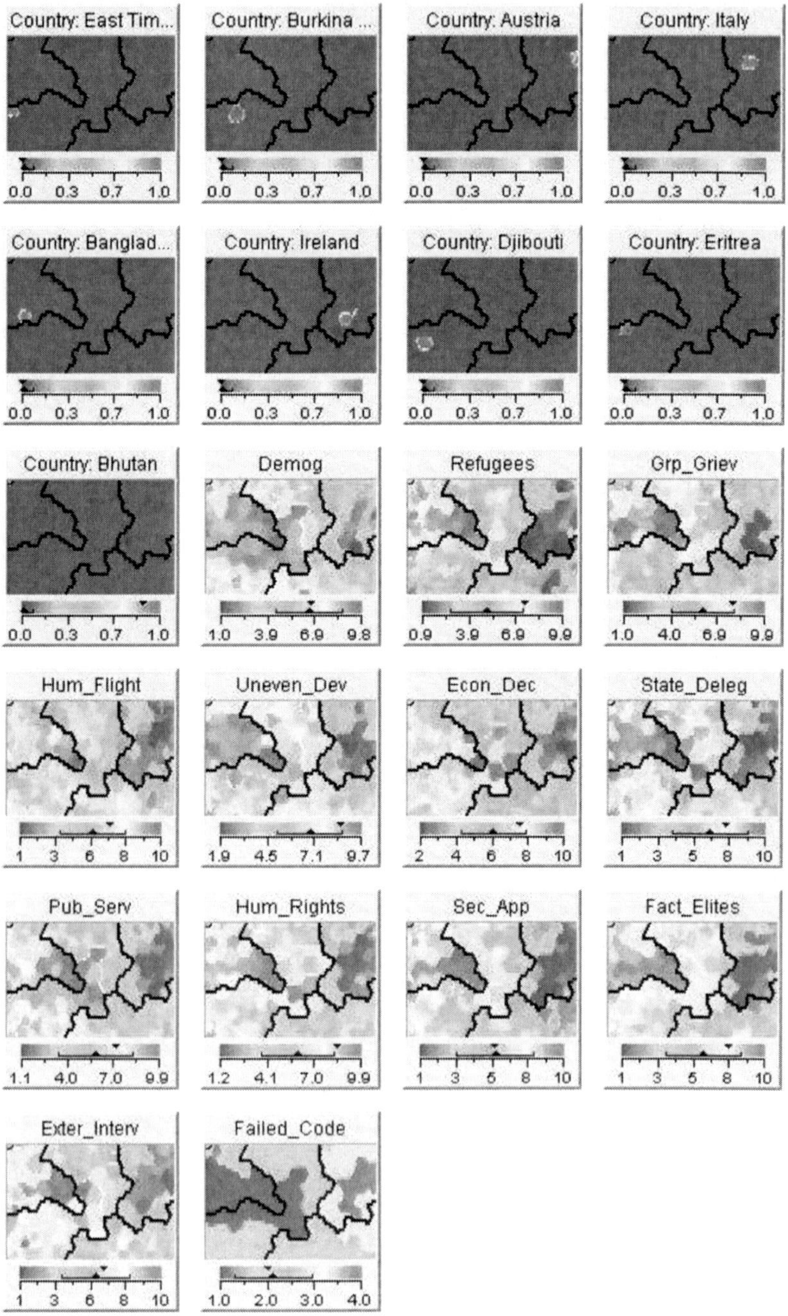

Figure 14. SOM temperature maps.

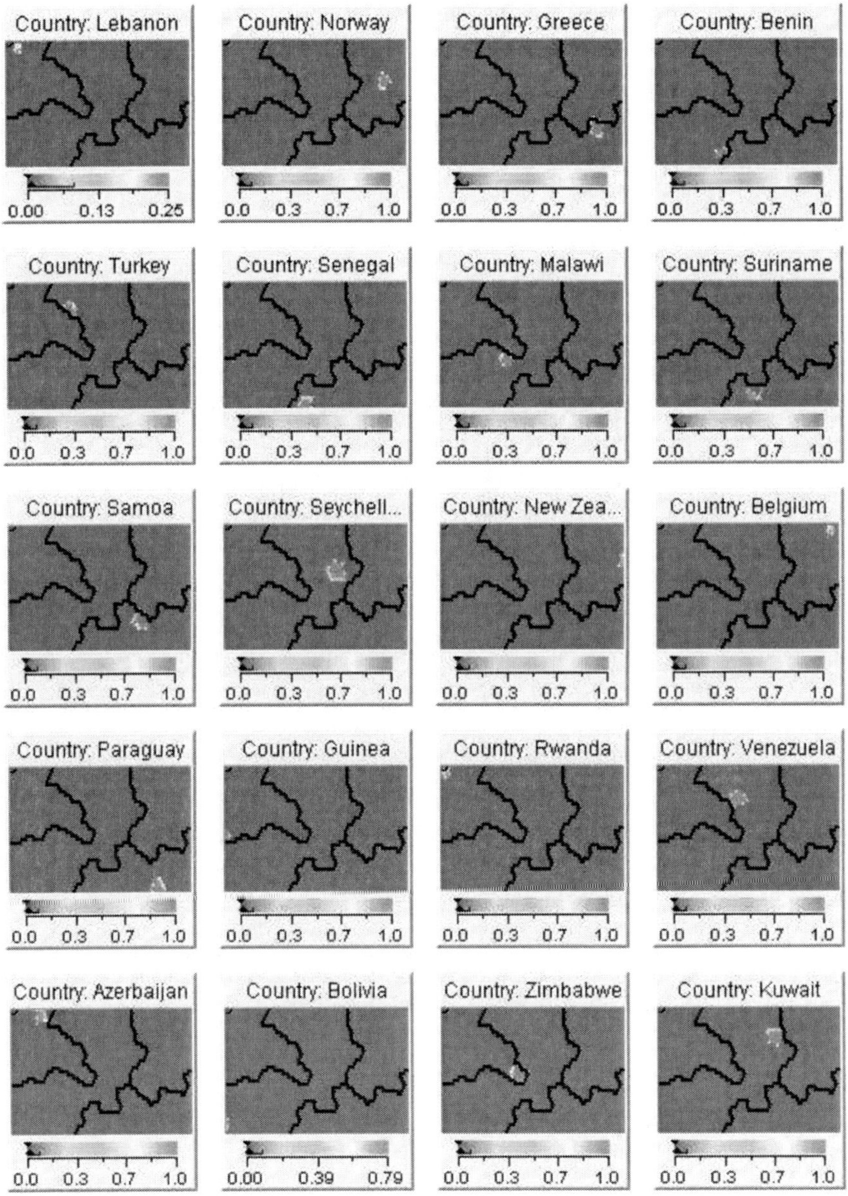

Figure 15. SOM prediction maps.

4. Implications, Limitations and Future Research

Our results confirm the theoretical work by Hecht-Nielson (1989) who has shown that computational intelligence models can learn input-output relationships to the point of making perfect forecasts with the data on which the network is trained. However, perfect forecasts with the training data do not guarantee optimal forecasts with the testing data due to differences in the two data sets. The good performance of these models in predicting and classifying failed states can be traced to its inherent non-linearity. This makes such techniques ideal for dealing with non-linear relations that may exist in the data. Thus, computational intelligence models are needed to better understand the inner dynamics of failed states at the global level. Our results are also in line with the findings of other researchers who have investigated the performance of neuro-computational models compared to other traditional statistical techniques, such as regression analysis, discriminant analysis, and logistic regression analysis. For example, in a study of clinical diagnosis of cancers, Shan et al., (2002) found a hit ratio of 85% for the neural network model compared to 80% for the LDA model. In a study of credit-scoring models used in commercial and consumer lending decisions, Bensic et al., (2005) compared the performance of logistic regression, neural networks and decision trees. The neural network model produced the highest hit rate and the lowest type I error. Similar findings have been reported in a study examining the performance of neural networks in predicting bankruptcy (Anandarajan et al., 2001) and diagnosis of acute appendicitis (Sakai et al., 2007).

Based on variable impact analysis, our findings imply that refugees may have a "billiard effect" on states failure. For example, the civil war in Liberia hastened the collapse of Sierra Leone, and the flow of refugees from Sierra Leone disrupted the unstable Guinean government. The Democratic Republic of Congo has rapidly collapsed in the aftermath of the Rwandan genocide. Our analysis also highlights the fact that declining democracy as manifested by a strong security apparatus is correlated with state failure. From both our SOM and variable impact analysis it is clear that states ruled by a strong security apparatus are far more likely to fail than stable democracies. We found that uneven development has an important impact on states' failure. This finding is in line with van de Walle's (2004) findings. Van de Walle argues that poorly executed macro-economic policies can lead to the failure of the state until the state ceases to provide virtually any public goods, and state agents become entirely predatory through rent seeking and corruption.

Despite the significant contributions of this study, it suffers from a number of limitations. First, this study has used a cross-sectional rather than a longitudinal approach. This implies that much more emphasis has been placed on observing failure across nations rather than in observing changes in states failure rates. There would seem to be hence a need for much more longitudinal research to focus on observing changes in states failure over time. Second, despite the satisfactory performance of the computational intelligence models in this study, future research might improve the performance of the models used in this study by integrating fuzzy discriminant analysis and genetic algorithms (GA) with computational intelligence models. Mirmirani and Li (2004) pointed out that traditional algorithms search for optimal weight vectors for a neural network with a given architecture, while GA can yield an efficient exploration of the search space when the modeler has little *apriori* knowledge of the structure of problem domains. Finally, future research might use other computational intelligence and evolutionary computation models' architectures such as gene expression programming (GEP) to classify and predict nations' failure. GEP was first introduced to the genetic programming (GP) community by Ferreira (2001). Thus, it is the most recent development in the field of artificial evolutionary systems (Ferreira, 2004). Due to the unsupervised character of their learning algorithm and the excellent visualization ability, GEP models have been recently used in myriad fields. Examples include particle physics data analysis (Teodorescu & Sherwood, 2008), food processing (Kahyaoglu, 2008), real parameter optimization (Xu et al., 2009), and chaotic maps analysis (Hardy & Steeb, 2002).

APPENDIX 1. R CODE USED TO IMPLEMENT SVM

```
fsi<-read.table("c:\\FSI.txt", header=T)
library(e1071)
 random.df<-sample(fsi)
 nobs<-nrow(fsi)
 n.test<-nobs %/% 10
test.df<-fsi[1:n.test,]
 diagnosis.df <- subset(test.df,select=Class)
 test.df<-subset(test.df, select=-Class)
 train.df<-fsi[(n.test+1):nobs,]
 cost.v<-c(0.01, 0.1, 1, 10, 100, 1000)
 error.cv<-c()
```

```
error.ho<-c()
for (i in cost.v)
{m.cv<-svm(Class~.,
data=fsi,
type="C-classification",
kernel="linear",
cost=i,
cross=10
)
e<-100 - summary(m.cv)$tot.accuracy
error.cv<-c(error.cv,e)
m.ho<-svm(Class ~.,
data=train.df,
type="C-classification",
kernel="linear",
cost=i,
cross=0
)
p<-predict(m.ho, test.df)
correct<-sum(p == diagnosis.df[[1]])
e<-(nrow(test.df) - correct)/nrow(test.df)*100
error.ho<-c(error.ho,e)
}
y<-max(error.ho, error.cv)
plot.new()
plot.window(xlim=c(1, length(cost.v)), ylim=c(0,y))
box()
title(xlab="SVM model complexity",ylab="Error rate")
xticks<-seq(1, length(cost.v),1)
yticks<-seq(0,y,1)
xlabels<-seq(1, length(cost.v),1)
ylabels<-seq(0,y,1)
axis(1,at=xticks,labels=xlabels)
axis(2,at=yticks,labels=ylabels)
points(1:length(cost.v),error.cv,type="b",col="red")
points(1:length(cost.v),error.ho,type="b",col="blue")
x<-fsi[, 2:13]
y<-fsi[, 14]
model<-svm(x, y)
```

```
print(model)
summary(model)
pred<-predict(model, x)
table(pred, y)
tobj<-tune.svm(Class~.,data=fsi[1:100,], gamma=10^(-6:-3),
cost=10^(1:2))
summary(tobj)
plot(tobj, transform.x = log10, xlab=expression(log[10](gamma)),
ylab="C")
```

APPENDIX 2. R CODE USED TO IMPLEMENT SOM

```
library(kohonen)
fsi<-read.table("c:\\FSI09.txt", header=T)
kohmap<-xyf(scale(fsi), classvec2classmat(Class), grid = somgrid(6, 6,
"hexagonal"), rlen=100)
plot(kohmap, type="changes" )
plot(kohmap, type="counts", main="Failed states data: counts")
plot(kohmap, type="quality", main="Failed states data: quality")
xyfpredictions<-classmat2classvec(predict(kohmap)$unit.predictions)
bgcols<-c("gray", "pink", "lightgreen")
plot(kohmap, type="mapping", col=Class+1, pchs=Class,
bgcol=bgcols[as.integer(xyfpredictions)], main = "mapping plot")
training<-sample(nrow(fsi), 100)
Xtraining<-scale(fsi[training, ])
Xtest<-scale(fsi[-training, ], center=attr(Xtraining, "scaled:center"),
scale=attr(Xtraining, "scaled:scale"))
som.fsi<-som(Xtraining, grid = somgrid(6, 6, "hexagonal"))
som.prediction<-predict(som.fsi, newdata = Xtest, trainX = Xtraining,
trainY = factor(Class [training]))
table(Class[-training], som.prediction$prediction)
```

REFERENCES

Aiken, M. & Bsat, M. (1999). Forecasting market trends with neural networks, *Information Systems Management*, 16: 42-49.

Aminian, F., Suarez, E., Aminian, M., & Walz, D. (2006). Forecasting economic data with neural networks. *Computational Economics*, 28, 71-88.

Anandarajan, M., Lee, P., & Anandarajan, A. (2001). Bankruptcy prediction of financially stressed firms: an examination of the predictive accuracy of artificial neural networks. *International Journal of Intelligent Systems in Accounting, Finance & Management*, 10, 69-81.

Audrain-Pontevia, A. (2006). Kohonen self-organizing maps: A neural approach for studying the links between attributes and overall satisfaction in a services context. *Journal of Consumer Satisfaction, Dissatisfaction and Complaining Behavior*, 19, 128-137.

Awad, M., & Motai, Y. (2008). Dynamic classification for video stream using support vector machine. *Applied Soft Computing*, 8, 1314-1325.

Balasubramanian, M., Palanivel, S. & Rmalingam, V. (2009). Real time face and mouth recognition using radial basis function neural networks. *Expert Systems with Applications*, 36, 6879-6888.

Bensic, M., Sarlija, N., & Zekic-Susac, M. (2005). Modelling small-business credit scoring by using logistic regression, neural networks and decision trees. *Intelligent Systems in Accounting, Finance and Management*, 13, 133-150.

Berrueta, L., Alonso-Salces, R., & Heberger, K. (2007). Supervised pattern recognition in food analysis. *Journal of Chromatography A*, 1158, 196-214.

Bishop, C. (2006). Pattern recognition and machine learning, 2nd edition, Springer, New York.

Calderon, T.,& Cheh, J. (2002). A roadmap for future neural networks research in auditing and risk assessment. *International Journal of Accounting Information Systems*, 3, 203-236.

Celikoglu, H., & Cigizoglu, H. (2007). Modeling public transport trips by radial basis function neural networks. *Mathematical and Computer Modeling*, 45, 480-489.

Chaplot, S., Patnaik, L., & Jagannathan, N. (2006). Classification of magnetic resonance brain images using wavlets as input to support vector machines and neural network. *Biomedical Signal Processing and Control*, 1, 86-92.

Chen, K., & Wang, C. (2007). A hybrid SARIMA and support vector machines in forecasting the production values of the machinery industry in Taiwan. *Expert Systems with Applications*, 32, 254-264.

Cheng, C., Chen, C. & Fu, C. (2006). Financial distress prediction by radial basis function network with logit analysis learning. *Computers and Mathematics with Applications*, 51, 579-588.

Child, D. (1990). *The Essentials of Factor Analysis*. Casell. London.

Churilov, L., & Flitman, A. (2006). Towards fair ranking of Olympics achievements: The case of Sydney 2000. *Computers & Operations Research*, 33, 2057-2082.

Coussement, K., & Van den Poel, D. (2008). Churn prediction in subscription services: An application of support vector machines while comparing two parameter-selection techniques. *Expert Systems with Applications*, 34, 313-327.

Darbellay, G. & Slama, M. (2000). forecasting the short-term demand for electricity: Do neural networks stand a better chance? *International Journal of Forecasting*, 16: 71-83.

Dhanalakshmi, P. Palanivel, S. & Ramalingam, (2009). Classification of audio signals using SVM and RBFNN. *Expert Systems with Applications*, 36, 6069-6075.

Dimitradou, E., Hornik, K., Leisch, F., Meyer, D., & Weingessel, A. (2005). E1071: Misc. functions of the Department of Statistics (e1071), TU Wein, Version 1.5-11. Available from http://cran.R-project.org.

Ding, C., & Patra, J. (2007). User modeling for personalized web search with self-organizing map. *Journal of the American Society for Information Science and Technology*, 58, 494-507.

Ferreira, C. (2001). Gene expression programming: a new adaptive algorithm for solving problems. *Complex Systems*, 13, 87-129.

Ferreira, C. (2004). Gene expression programming and the evolution of computer programs. In Leonardo de Castro and Fernando Von Zuben (Eds.). *Recent Developments in biologically inspired computing*. Idea Group Publishing, pp. 82-103.

Foreign Policy (2009). The failed states index, 80-83 (July/August).

Frota, R., Barreto, G., & Mota, J. (2007). Anomaly detection in mobile communication network using the self-organizing map. *Journal of Intelligent and Fuzzy Systems*, 18, 493-500.

Fund for Peace (FundForPeace.org).

Ghaziri, H. & Osman, I. (2006). Self-organizing feature maps for the vehicle routing problem with backhauls. *Journal of Scheduling*, 9, 97-114.

Gorr, W., Nagin, D., & Szczypula, J. (1994). comparative study of artificial neural network and statistical models for predicting student point averages, *International Journal of Forecasting*, 10: 17-34.

Hair, J., Anderson, R., Tatham, R. & Black, W. (1998). Multivariate data analysis with readings.

Hardy, Y., & Steeb, W. (2002). Gene expression programming and one-dimensional chaotic maps. *International Journal of Modern Physics C*, 13-24.

Harvey, C., Travers, K., & Costa, M. (2000). Forecasting emerging market returns using neural networks, *Emerging Markets Quarterly*, 4: 43-55.

Hecht-Nielson, R. (1989). *Theory of the back-propagation neural network.* International Joint Conference on Neural Networks. Washington, DC, 593-605.

Hehir, A. (2007). The myth of the failed state and the war on terror: a challenge to the conventional wisdom. *Journal of Intervention and state Building*, 1, 307-332.

Helman, G., & Ratner, S. (1993). Saving failed states. Foreign Policy, 89, 3-21.

Howard, T. (2008). Revisiting state failure: developing a causal model of state failure based upon theoretical insight. *Civil Wars*, 10, 125-147.

Iyer, S. & Sharda, R. (2009). Prediction of athletes' performance using neural networks: an application in cricket team selection. *Expert Systems with Applications*, 36, 5510-5522.

Jiang, E. (2007). Detecting spam email by radial basis function networks. *International Journal of Knowledge-based and Engineering Systems*, 11, 409-418.

Kahyaoglu, T. (2008). Optimization of the pistachio nut roasting process using response surface methodology and gene expression programming. *LWT-Food Science and Technology*, 41, 26-33.

Kaiser, H. (1970). A second generation little jiffy. *Psychometrika*, 35, 401-415.

Karatzoglou, A., Meyer, D., & Hornik, K. (2005). Support vector machines in R. Available at http://statmath.wu-wien.ac.at.

Kecman, V. (2005). Support vector machines: An introduction. In L. Wang (Ed.), Support vector machines: Theory and applications. Springer-Verlag, Berlin, 1-48.

Kim, J., & Mueller, C. (1978). *Introduction to Factor Analysis*. Sage Publications. Beverly Hills. CA.

Koetz, B., Morsdorf, F., Linden, S., Curt, T., & Allgower, B. (2008). Multi-source land cover classification for forest management based on imaging spectrometry and LIDAR data. *Forest Ecology and Management*, 256, 263-271.

Kohonen, T. (1982). Self-organized formation of topologically correct feature maps. *Biological Cybernetics*, 43, 59-69.

Kohonen, T. (2001). Self-organizing maps. 3rd Ed., Springer, Berlin.

Kohzadi, N., Boyd, M., Kemlanshahi, B., & Kaastra, I. (1996). A Comparison of artificial neural network and time series models for forecasting commodity prices, *Neurocomputing*, 10: 169-181.

Kumar, K., & Bhattacharya, S. (2006). Artificial neural network vs. linear discriminant analysis in credit ratings forecast. *Review of Accounting and Finance*, 5, 216-227.

Kuo, R., Ho, L., & Hu, C. (2002). Integration of self-organizing feature map and K-means algorithm for market segmentation. *Computers & Operations Research*, 29, 1475-1493.

Lambach, D. (2004). The perils of weakness: failed states and perceptions of threat in Europe and Australia. Paper presented at the New Security Agendas Conference. Kings College, London, July 1-3.

Lapedes, A. & Farber, R. (1988). How neural nets work? In Anderson, D. (Ed). *Neural information processing systems*, American Institute of Physics, New York: 442-456.

Lek, S., & Guegan, J. (1999).Artificial neural networks as a tool in ecological modelling: an introduction. *Ecological Modeling*, 120, 65-73.

Lemarchand, R. (2003). The Democratic Republic of Congo: from failure to potential reconstruction. In Robert. I. Rotberg (ed). State failure and state weakness in a time of terror. World Peace Foundation, Washington, DC, 29-70.

Li, X., Zhou, J., Yuan, S., Zhou, X., & Fu, Q. (2008). Using support vector machines to predict eco-environmental burden. *Biomedical and Environmental Sciences*, 21, 45-52.

Lim, C., & Kirikoshi, T. (2005). Predicting the effects of physician-directed promotion on prescription yield and sales uptake using neural networks. *Journal of Targeting, Measurement and Analysis for Marketing*, 13, 158-167.

Liu, H., Wen, Y., & Gao, Y. (2009). Application of experimental design and radial basis function neural network to the separation and determination of active components in traditional Chinese medicines by capillary electrophoresis. *Analytica Chimica Acta*, 638, 88-93.

Lo, Z., & Bavarian, B. (1993). Analysis of convergence properties of topology preserving neural networks. *IEEE Transactions on Neural Networks*, 11, 207-220.

Luan, F., Liu, T., Wen, Y., & Zhang, X. (2008). Classification of the fragrance properties of chemical compounds based on support vector machine and linear discriminant analysis. *Flavor and Fragrance Journal*, 23, 232-238.

Mahdi, A. (2006). Perceptual non-intrusive speech quality assessment using a self-organizing map. *Journal of Enterprise Information Management*, 19, 148-164.

McMenamin, J. & Monforte, F. (1998). Short term energy forecasting with neural networks, *Energy Journal*, 19: 43-52.

Melssen, W., Wehrens, R., & Buydens, L. (2006). Supervised Kohonen networks for classification problems. *Chemometrics and Intelligent Laboratory Systems*, 83, 99-113.

Mirmirani, S., & Li, H. (2004). Gold price, neural networks and genetic algorithm. *Computational Economics*, 23, 193-200.

Moreno, D., Marco, P., and Olmeda, I. (2006). Self-organizing maps could improve the classification of Spanish mutual funds. *European Journal of Operational Research*, 147, 1039-1054.

Mostafa, M. (2009). Shades of green: a psychographic segmentation of the green consumer in Kuwait using self-organizing maps", *Expert Systems with Applications*, 36, 11030-11038.

Nam, K. & Yi, J. (1997). Predicting airline passenger volume, *Journal of Business Forecasting Methods & Systems*, 16: 14-17.

Piazza, J. (2008). Incubators of terror: do failed and failing states promote transnational terrorism? *International Studies Quarterly*, 52, 469-488.

Poh, H. Yao, J. & Jasic, T. (1998). Neural networks for the analysis and forecasting of advertising impact, *International Journal of Intelligent Systems in Accounting, Finance & management*, 7: 253-268.

Prentice Hall (Englewood Cliffs, NJ).

Reno, W. (2003). Sierra Leone: warfare in a post-state sooociety. In Robert. I. Rotberg (ed). State failure and state weakness in a time of terror. World Peace Foundation, Washington, DC, 71-100.

Ruiz-Suarez, J., Mayora -Ibarra, O., Torres -Jimenez, J., & Ruiz-Suarez, L. (1995). Short term ozone forecasting by artificial neural network, *Advances in Engineering Software*, 23: 143-149.

Sakai, S., Kobayashi, K., Toyabe, S., Mandai, N., Kanda, T., & Akazawa, K. (2007). Comparison of the levels of accuracy of an artificial neural network model and a logistic regression model for the diagnosis of acute appendicitis. *Journal of Medical Systems*. 31, 357-364.

Shan, Y., Zhao, R., Xu, G., Liebich., & Zhang, Y. (2002). Application of probabilistic neural network in the clinical diagnosis of cancers based on clinical chemistry data. *Analytica Chimica Acta*, 471, 77-86.

Siew, E., Smith, K., Churilov, L., & Ibrahim, M. (2002). A neural clustering approach for Iso-Resource groupings for acute healthcare in Australia. Proceedings of the 35th Annual Hawaii International Conference on Systems Science (HICS35). IEEE Computer Society, Hawaii, USA.

Silven, O., Niskanen, M., & Kauppinen, H. (2003). Wood inspection with non supervised clustering. *Machine Vision and Applications*, 13, 275-285.

Silver, H., & Shmoish, M. (2008). Analysis of cognitive performance in schizophrenia patients and healthy individuals with unsupervised clustering models. *Psychiatry Research*, 159, 167-179.

SPSS Neural Networks Version 17.0, SPSS Corporation (2007).

Stavrou, E., Spiliotis, S., & Charalambpuw, C. (2010). Flexible working arrangements in context : an empirical investigation through self-organising maps. *European Journal of Operational Research*, 202, 893-902.

Swicegood, P., & Clark, J. (2001). Off-site monitoring systems for prediction bank underperformance: a comparison of neural networks, discriminant analysis, and professional human judgment. *International Journal of Intelligent Systems in Accounting, Finance & Management*, 10, 169-186.

Teodorescu, L. & Sherwood, D. (2008). High energy physics event selection with gene expression programming. *Computer Physics Communications*, 178, 409-419.

Thneberg, H., & Hotulainen, R. (2006). Contributions of data mining for psycho-educational research: What self-organizing maps tell us about the well-being of gifted learners. *High Ability Studies*, 17, 87-100.

Van de Walle, N. (2004). The economic correlates of state failure: taxes, foreign aid and policies. In Robert I. Rotberg (ed). When states fail: causes and consequences. Princeton University Press, 94-115.

Vapnik, V. (1995). The nature of statistical learning theory. Springer, Berlin.

Vesanto, J. & Alhoniemi, E. (2000). Clustering of the self-organizing map. *IEEE Transactions on Neural Networks*, 11, 586-600.

Vesanto, J. (1999). SOM-based data visualisation methods. *Intelligent Data Analysis*, 3, 111-126.

Videnova, I., Nedialkova, D., Dimitrova, M., & Popova, S. (2006). Neural networks for air pollution forecasting. *Applied Artificial Intelligence*, 20, 493-506.

Vijayakumar, C., Damayanti, G., Pant, R. & Sreedhar, C. (2007). Segmentation and grading of brain tumors on apparent diffusion coefficient images using self-organizing maps. *Computerized Medical Imaging and Graphics*, 31, 473-484.

Viscovery Software GmbH (2008), SOMine user's manual version 5.0, Vienna, Austria.

Wang, S. (1995). The unpredictability of standard back propagation neural networks in classification applications. *Management Science*, 41, 555-559.

Wehrens, R., & Buydens, L. (2007). Self- and super-organizing maps in R: the Kohonen package. *Journal of Statistical Software*, 21 (5).

Worner, S., & Gevrey, M. (2006). Modeling global insect pest species assemblages to determine risk of invasion. *Journal of Applied Ecology*, 43, 858-867.

Xu, K., Liu, Y., Tang, R., Zuo, J., & Tang, C. (2009). A novel method for real parameter optimization based on gene expression programming. *Applied Soft Computing*, 9, 725-737.

Yan, A. (2006). Application of self-organizing maps in compounds pattern recognition and combinatorial library design. *Combinatorial Chemistry & High Throughput Screening*, 9, 473-480.

Yu, B., & Xu, Z. (2008). A comparative study for content-based dynamic spam classification using four machine learning algorithms. *Knowledge-Based Systems*, 21, 355-362.

Zartman, W. (1995). Collapsed States: The disintegration and restoration of legitimate authority. Lynne Rienner, Boulder, CO.

Zhong, S., Khoshgoftaar, M., & Seliya, N. (2007). Clustering-based network intrusion detection. *International Journal of Reliability, Quality and Safety Engineering*, 14, 169-187.

Zhuang, Z., Churilov, L., Burstein, F., & Sikaris, K. (2009). Combining data mining and case-based reasoning for intelligent decision support for pathology ordering by general practitioners. *European Journal of Operational Research*, 195, 662-675.

Zhuo, W., Li-Min, J., Yong, Q., & Yan-hui, W. (2007). Railway passenger traffic volume prediction based on neural network. *Applied Artificial Intelligence*, 21, 1-10.

In: Data Mining
Editor: Harold L. Capri
ISBN: 978-1-63463-738-1

Chapter 4

AN EVOLUTIONARY SELF-ADAPTIVE ALGORITHM FOR MINING ASSOCIATION RULES

José María Luna[1,*], ***Alberto Cano***[1,†] ***and Sebastián Ventura***[1,2,‡]
[1]Dept. of Computer Science and Numerical Analysis,
University of Cordoba
[2]Dept. of Computer Science, King Abdulaziz University,
Saudi Arabia Kingdom

Abstract

This paper presents a novel self-adaptive grammar-guided genetic programming proposal for mining association rules. It generates individuals through a context-free grammar, which allows of defining rules in an expressive and flexible way over different domains. Each rule is represented as a derivation tree that shows a solution (described using the language) denoted by the grammar. Unlike existing evolutionary algorithms for mining association rules, the proposed algorithm only requires a small number of parameters, providing the possibility of discovering association rules in an easy way for non-expert users. More specifically, this algorithm does not require any threshold, and uses a novel parent selector based on a niche-crowding model to group rules. This approach keeps the

*E-mail address: jmluna@uco.es
†E-mail address: acano@uco.es
‡E-mail address: sventura@uco.es (Corresponding author)

best individuals in a pool and restricts the extraction of similar rules by analysing the instances covered.

We compare our approach with the G3PARM algorithm, the first grammar-guided genetic programming algorithm for the extraction of association rules. G3PARM was described as a high-performance algorithm, obtaining important results and overcoming the drawbacks of current exhaustive search and evolutionary algorithms. Experimental results show that our new proposal obtains very interesting and reliable rules with higher support values.

Keywords: Association rules; grammar guided genetic grogramming; evolutionary computation; self-adaptive operators

1. Introduction

Association rule mining (ARM), an important area of data mining, has received enormous attention since its introduction by Agrawal et al. [1, 2] in the early 90s. ARM searches for strong relationships among items that are hidden in datasets. An association rule (AR) is defined as an implication of the form $Antecedent \rightarrow Consequent$, both $Antecedent$ and $Consequent$ being sets with no items in common. The meaning of an AR is that if the antecedent is satisfied, then it is highly probable that the consequent will be also satisfied.

Most existing proposals for the extraction of ARs follow an exhaustive search methodology based on a support–confidence framework [2, 6, 35], where the support calculates the proportion of transactions covered by the rule, and the confidence specifies how reliable the rule is. In these proposals, frequent patterns are mined first, and are next used to extract reliable ARs. The mining process is hindered by these two steps, which require a large amount of computational time and large amounts of memory. Notice that with the growing interest in the storage of information, real-world datasets containing numerical values have turned out to be essential to the research community. Since numerical domains typically contain many distinct values, the search space in these domains is bigger than the search space in categorical domains. In such situations, exhaustive search algorithms in ARM cannot directly deal with numerical domains as they become hardly maintainable.

Evolutionary algorithms (EA) have been widely used in data mining tasks, where the process of searching for solutions requires an optimization. Many researchers have focused on the ARM problems from an evolutionary perspective [22, 24], facing up to the exhaustive search approaches' computational and memory requirements. Most of these existing evolutionary approaches are based on genetic algorithms (GA) [4, 33], having a fixed-length chromosome that is not very flexible at all. A technique based on EA is genetic programming (GP) [11, 18], the individual representation being its main peculiarity. In GP, solutions are represented with variable-length hierarchical structures, usually in a tree form, where the size, shape and structural complexity are not constrained a priori [13].

Recently, an ARM algorithm was proposed [21] which was based on G3P (Grammar Guided Genetic Programming) [25], an extension of GP. It was presented as the first G3P proposal for mining ARs, providing great results and overcoming those drawbacks of current ARM algorithms in terms of its execution time, the mining of numerical domains, and solution complexity. This algorithm, called G3PARM (Grammar Guided Genetic Programming Association Rule Mining), makes use of a grammar to constrain the GP process, promoting the creation of individuals with valid syntax forms. Each solution given by G3PARM satisfies the language defined by the grammar, which allowed of obtaining solutions over different domains. G3PARM was originally described as a fully configurable algorithm, where a number of input parameters were required, e.g., support and confidence thresholds, crossover and mutation probabilities, the number of generations, the population size, etc. This kind of algorithms is highly recommended in many situations, especially when they are used by qualified data miners. Nevertheless, the possibility of mining ARs using a high-performance algorithm without the need to specify a large number of parameters is a requirement for non-expert users.

In this paper, the G3PARM+ algorithm, an interesting self-adaptive G3P algorithm, is proposed for mining ARs. This proposal also uses a context-free grammar (CFG) to define syntax constraints and extract rules in both numerical and categorical domains. During its evolutionary process, the proposal discovers ARs by applying two genetic operators over those rules selected as parents by means of a niche-crowding [9, 10] model. Both genetic operators adjust their probabilities along the mining process. The proposed algorithm allows of obtaining ARs without any previous knowledge of the dataset, and does not require support or confidence thresholds. Moreover, a support–confidence framework is not purely accomplished, bringing the lift measure into play in order to extract frequent, reliable, and also interesting rules. The resulting set of rules comprises dissimilar rules, covering a high percentage of the dataset instances, which is measured by the coverage. It is noteworthy that for the sake of avoiding mismatched rules, the instances covered by each rule are analysed. The results clarify the good behaviour and efficiency of this proposal compared to G3PARM, which was previously contrasted to other exhaustive and genetic algorithms in [21]. More specifically, the empirical comparison demonstrates that the new proposal obtains interesting rules with high support, high confidence, and high coverage of dataset instances.

This paper is structured as follows: the main drawbacks of the support-confidence framework are discussed and the most relevant related work is presented in Section 2; Section 3 describes the model proposed as well as its main characteristics; Section 4 describes the experiments, including the datasets used, the algorithm set-up, and disucsses the results obtained; finally, in Section 5, some concluding remarks are outlined.

2. Preliminaries

The support–confidence framework is the most often used combination of measures in the ARM field. Actually, most existing proposals use the support measure for mining frequent patterns, whereas the confidence measure is used for discovering reliable rules. As discussed next, new measures are required in the extraction of interesting ARs, since the use of the support–confidence framework becomes insufficient. Finally, the most relevant ARM proposals are described. The first proposals were designed following an exhaustive search methodology. Currently, the use of exhaustive search methods is not a good option and evolutionary ARM proposals are the most studied.

2.1. The Support–confidence Framework

Different measures have been proposed to evaluate the quality of the rules extracted in the ARM process [3, 12, 23, 27]. Support and confidence [19] are two measures which are well-known to the research community. The former (sup) is defined in Equation 1 as the proportion of the number of transactions T including the antecedent A and the consequent C in a dataset record collection D. The latter *conf* is defined in Equation 2 as the proportion of the number of transactions which include A and C among all the transactions that include A.

$$sup(A \rightarrow C) = \frac{|\{A \cup C \subseteq T, T \in D\}|}{|D|} \quad (1)$$

$$conf(A \rightarrow C) = \frac{sup(A \rightarrow C)}{sup(A)} \quad (2)$$

A great variety of proposals in ARM make use of this support–confidence framework [2, 6, 14, 28, 35]. These proposals attempt to discover rules whose support and confidence values are greater than certain thresholds. However, the mere fact of having rules that exceed these thresholds does not guarantee that the rules are interesting at all, as described in [12]. Even when the support and confidence thresholds are satisfied by a rule, if this AR acquires a confidence value less than its consequent support, then the rule is misleading. The occurrence of the antecedent does not imply an increment in the occurrence of the consequent.

For a better understanding, suppose that there are ten customers in a market. Five of them bought bread, six bought milk, and two bought both bread and milk, as shown in Table 1. Attending to the confidence measure, which serves to calculate how much a given product depends on another, two out of five customers that bought bread bought milk too, i.e., 40% of them. On the other hand, the expected confidence represents the proportion of the occurrences of one element independently of another, the expected confidence of buying milk being six out of ten, i.e., 60% of the customers. So the probability of buying milk is greater than the probability of the event of buying bread too, and hence the association provides a negative dependence. Studying the number of customers

Table 1. Sample market customers

Customer	Bread	Milk	Coffee
Id-1	1	1	1
Id-2	0	1	0
Id-3	1	0	0
Id-4	1	0	0
Id-5	0	1	0
Id-6	1	1	1
Id-7	0	1	0
Id-8	1	0	0
Id-9	0	1	1
Id-10	0	0	1

that bought milk and coffee, 40% of the customers bought coffee, whereas three out of six customers that bought milk bought coffee too, i.e., 50% of them. In this situation, the fact of buying milk provides a positive expectation for the event of buying coffee. Finally, two out of five customers that bought bread bought coffee too, i.e., 40% of them, while four out of ten customers bought coffee independently of anything else, i.e., 40% of the customers. Thus, the fact of buying bread does not provide any information about the event of buying coffee, neither positive nor negative, so the association relates independent events.

These three possibilities may occur when using support and confidence measures, which makes necessary the use of a third measure to bring more effective information to the data mining task. The interest or lift measure [7], defined in Equation 3, serves to calculate how many times more often the antecedent and consequent are related in a dataset than would be expected if they were statistically independent.

$$lift(A \rightarrow C) = \frac{conf(A \rightarrow C)}{sup(C)} \tag{3}$$

While lift values greater than unity are desired, which would mean that there exists a positive dependence between the antecedent and consequent, lift values less than or equal to unity, i.e., the confidence value is lower than the consequent support, provide misleading rules. The interest of mining ARs over frequent patterns lies in the extraction of rules with high support, i.e., those that satisfy many dataset instances. However, the discovery of rules with maximal support, e.g., those that cover all the dataset instances, does not provide any new information and so is normally not interesting.

Note that lift is not the extent of the problem. In our opinion, a main drawback of this measure is that its range is not bounded, i.e., its domain is $[0, \infty)$. In consequence, it is not trivial to compare the values of several rules by only using the lift measure, since differences between them are not informative.

Another important measure to bear in mind in the ARM field is the coverage measure, $cover$, which is defined in Equation 4. This measure evaluates the quality of the set of rules $(R_1, R_2, ...R_n)$ discovered in the mining process, calculating the percentage of instances covered by this set. The higher is this measure, the more representative is the set of rules.

$$cover(R_1, R_2, ...R_n) = \frac{|\{R_1, R_2, ...R_n \subseteq T, T \in D\}|}{|D|} \tag{4}$$

In the present paper, we propose to apply the support, confidence and lift measures at the same time to determine the quality of the rules mined. Additionally, it is interesting to discover a representative set of rules, not only rules having high quality, so the coverage measure is used to determine the percentage of instances covered by the resulting set of rules. Finally, since the quality of the rules is calculated by using support, confidence and lift all at once, it is necessary to clarify the relationship between them.

Focusing on the support and confidence measures, notice that the confidence of a rule is greater than or equal to its support (see Equation 5), and its value is a maximum if the instances covered by the antecedent of an AR is a subset of the instances covered by the consequent of the rule. In addition, the confidence measure is symmetric iff $sup(A) = sup(C)$.

$$conf(A \rightarrow C) \geq sup(A \rightarrow C) \tag{5}$$

On the other hand, focusing on the lift measure and having a maximal confidence value, the lift value is greater than unity if the consequent does not satisfy all the dataset instances. Besides, if the antecedent or consequent satisfies all the dataset instances, both the antecedent and consequent are independent and, therefore, the rule is misleading. As is stated in Equation 6, the lift value has an inverse relationship to the concept of support.

$$lift(A \rightarrow C) \leq \frac{1}{sup(A \rightarrow C)} \tag{6}$$

In addition, lift is related to the confidence measure, as depicted in Equation 7. Here, the maximum lift value is determined by the dataset size if the confidence is maximum.

$$lift(A \rightarrow C) \leq |D| * conf(A \rightarrow C) \tag{7}$$

Finally, note that the support and lift measures are symmetric, i.e., $sup(A \rightarrow C) = sup(C \rightarrow A)$ and $lift(A \rightarrow C) = lift(C \rightarrow A)$ for every value of A and C. On the other hand, this property is not present in the confidence measure.

2.2. Existing ARM Algorithms

The first proposals for mining ARs were based on that presented by *Agrawal* [1], where the problem of discovering ARs was divided into two steps. The former extracts patterns that frequently appear in a dataset, which requires much computational time, which grows with the number of available attributes. The latter discovers ARs using only those frequent patterns previously obtained.

Thereafter, many algorithms were presented based on *Agrawal*'s proposal. The main motivation of these algorithms is the reduction of the computational time and the memory requirements. A significant example is the Eclat algorithm [34], which represents the dataset as a bit matrix, where each row represents an item and each column represents a transaction. Within the bit matrix, each bit is set if the item is satisfied, otherwise it is cleared. In this algorithm, a depth-first strategy is applied, obtaining candidate items. In order to obtain a new item comprising two items previously mined, the intersection of their bits in the matrix is found to check whether they have common bits. This new candidate set is added to the bit matrix if it satisfies a minimum number of transactions.

Han et al.[14] proposed FP-Growth, which makes use of a frequent pattern tree (FP-tree) structure, i.e., an extended prefix-tree structure storing information about frequent patterns. In its pattern mining process, the algorithm works on the FP-tree instead of the whole dataset, employing a divide-and-conquer method to reduce the computational time. Recently, an improvement of FP-Growth was presented in [17]. This proposal, called IFP-Growth (Improved FP-Growth), uses a novel structure, called FP-tree+, and an address table to decrease the complexity of building the entire FP-tree. Both the FP-tree+ and the address table require lower memory requirements but provide a better performance in comparison with the algorithm originally proposed by Han et al.

Although these algorithms were designed to overcome the problems mentioned above, it should be noted that all of them follow an exhaustive search approach, and so still have important drawbacks such as their computational time and memory requirements. Furthermore, a bad choice in the value of the support threshold may produce a towering number of ARs. More specifically, the use of traditional support–confidence thresholds could produce a large number of irrelevant or even misleading ARs [30]. Finally, it should be noted that only categorical patterns could be mined, so numerical attributes have to be previously discretized. Nowadays, the overcoming of these problems is still under study. Currently, these issues are mainly addressed by using EA [4, 5, 24, 33], where EA and, particularly, GA are especially appropriate when the search space is too large to apply an exhaustive search method. An important issue with these EAs is the ability of mining ARs without requiring a previous extraction of frequent patterns.

The search for ARs over datasets comprising numerical attributes is also interesting to many data mining experts [4, 22, 29, 31]. Some researches use a GA to optimize intervals on a set of rules previously computed, e.g., QuantMiner [29]. In the initial population, each numerical attribute is represented by means of intervals defining the whole domain, and then the length of these intervals is decreased until the minimum support threshold is reached. Sometimes, the necessity of using numerical ARs along with positive and negative conditions have led to different studies, such as the one by Alatas et al.[4]. They proposed an EA where each chromosome is composed of genes representing items and their intervals, where the ith item is encoded by the ith gene, and each one comprises four parts. The former provides three values that indicate if a certain item belongs to the antecedent, the consequent or, on the contrary, is not present in the rule. The second part represents whether the item is positive or negative. The last two parts represent the upper and lower bounds of the interval. In consecuence, for m attributes in a dataset, each chromosome comprises $m * 4$ genes. Alatas et al. proposed a fitness function to decide the amplitude of the intervals, providing several parameters to increase or decrease the effects of the different parts of the fitness function. Even though these algorithms obtained important results, they mine rules only over numerical attributes, this issue being an important drawback.

Another relevant proposal is ARMGA (Association Rule Mining Genetic Algorithm) [33], which encodes each AR as a single chromosome. This algorithm numbers all the dataset items by using their indices $(i_1, i_2, ..., i_n)$. The first gene is an indicator that separates the antecedent from the consequent in the chromosome, while the next genes represent each of the items. So, a length-k rule is represented by $k + 1$ genes. The fitness function F_{ARMGA} used in this proposal is the relative confidence (see Equation 8). In order to obtain new individuals in a given generation of the evolutionary process, two genetic operators are defined: the crossover operator uses a two-point strategy; the mutator changes those genes in the chromosome that exceed a certain probability.

$$F_{ARMGA} = \frac{sup(A \rightarrow C) - sup(A)sup(C)}{sup(A)(1 - sup(C))} \quad (8)$$

Notice that GA represents every chromosome with a fixed-length, which is not flexible at all. On the other hand, in GP, each solution is represented by a tree-form variable-length hierarchical structure. An extension of GP, the G3P methodology, allows of applying syntax constraints to GP trees by means of a CFG, each individual being a derivation tree. The use of grammars becomes interesting in defining valid expressions when their restrictions are known. Each tree is built up by applying production rules and a maximum tree depth is specified to avoid very deep trees.

Recently, a promising algorithm based on G3P was proposed [21]. In this algorithm, called G3PARM, the searching process is constrained by using a grammar. G3PARM works by maximizing the support and confidence measures in order to discover the best rules in a dataset. An important feature of G3PARM is that it provides an auxiliary population with a predefined size to keep the best rules, those that exceed the thresholds mentioned above. This auxiliary population is only completed if enough rules satisfy these thresholds, so fewer rules than those expected by the data miner could be mined.

This high-performance algorithm requires a number of parameters that should be established by an expert, e.g., support and confidence thresholds, crossover and mutation probabilities, or the number of rules to be extracted. Nevertheless, there are situations where the number of parameters and the need for previous knowledge of the dataset impose important drawbacks. Under these circumstances, a self-adaptive algorithm is appropriate, not requiring a huge number of parameters, e.g. specific support and confidence thresholds. There are already some previous genetic algorithms in the literature [15, 16] which have tackled the problem of self-adapting their parameters. Nevertheless, notice that the synergy of using a self-adaptation model together with the advantages of G3P brings about an interesting model for mining highly frequent and reliable association rules.

3. G3PARM+

This proposal mines ARs requiring only a few parameters and uses G3P to define ARs whose syntax is conformant to a CFG. Each derivation tree is evaluated by applying two criteria. One guides the search for solutions along the mining process. The other one allows of selecting the best solutions found. To mine new individuals in the evolutionary process, a parent selector using a niche-crowding methodology and two new genetic operators are presented.

G = $(\Sigma_N, \Sigma_T, P, S)$ with:

S = AssociationRule
Σ_N = {AssociationRule, Antecedent, Consequent, Condition, Categorical Operator, Categorical Values, Numerical Values}
Σ_T = {'AND', '! =', '=', 'IN', 'OUT', 'CategoricalAttribute', 'CategoricalValue', 'NumericalAttribute', 'NumericalValue'}
P = {AssociationRule = Antecedent, Consequent ;
Antecedent = Condition | 'AND', Condition, Antecedent ;
Consequent = Condition | 'AND', Condition, Consequent;
Condition = Categorical Operator, Categorical Value | Numerical Operator, Numerical Value ;}
Categorical Operator = '! =' | '=' ;
Numerical Operator = 'IN' | 'OUT' ;
Categorical Value = 'CategoricalAttribute' 'CategoricalValue';
Numerical Value = 'NumericalAttribute' 'NumericalValue' 'NumericalValue'; }

Figure 1. Context-free grammar expressed in extended BNF notation.

3.1. Encoding Criterion

In this proposal, each individual is defined by a genotype and a phenotype. The former is defined by means of a tree structure with different shapes and sizes. The latter represents the AR defined by the tree structure. This tree structure is obtained according to the definition of a CFG G, which is defined as shown in Figure 1.

A CFG is defined as a four-tuple $(\Sigma_N, \Sigma_T, P, S)$, Σ_N being the non-terminal symbol alphabet, Σ_T denoting the terminal symbol alphabet, P standing for the set of production rules, S for the start symbol, and Σ_N and Σ_T being disjoint sets (i.e., $\Sigma_N \cap \Sigma_T = \emptyset$). Any production rule follows the format $\alpha \rightarrow \beta$ where $\alpha \in \Sigma_N$, and $\beta \in \{\Sigma_T \cup \Sigma_N\}^*$. Beginning from the start symbol S, each individual is represented in a derivation syntax-tree as a sentence conformant to the grammar.

To obtain individuals, a set of derivation steps is carried out by applying the production rules declared in the set P and starting from the start symbol, AssociationRule. Once the tree is defined through the application of production rules, and in order to obtain the individual representation, a pre-order traversal of the tree is performed from the start symbol. Notice that each terminal symbol adopts the names and values of any of the dataset attributes. Using the sample metadata from Table 2, the terminal symbol Condition could adopt any attribute such as toy, toy's price, or sex. Once the attribute is assigned, a ran-

Table 2. A sample metadata

Attributes	**Values**
toy	ball, teddy, doll
toy's price	[10, 50]
sex	male, female

dom value is selected in the domain of such attribute, e.g., ball, teddy, or doll for the attribute toy.

The proposal here presented allows the use of both categorical and numerical attributes. In a sample AR, a categorical attribute accepts a value in a discrete unordered domain D. Given an attribute x and a value y in the domain D of x, both the expression $x = y$ and $x \; ! = y$ are permitted. The expression $x \; ! = y$ indicates that x takes any value in $D \backslash \{y\}$. On the other hand, numerical attributes are used by applying the operators IN or OUT and randomly selecting two feasible values.

For the sake of clarifying the individual representation, it is interesting to show a sample individual generated through the application of a sequence of production rules from P (see Figure 2). The terminal nodes were obtained from the sample meta-data aforementioned. The categorical condition 'toy = ball' could be obtained this way, as well as the numerical condition 'toy's price IN [25, 43]'. Therefore, according to the sample tree obtained from the sample dataset, the phenotype would represent the following rule:

IF $toy'sprice \; IN \; [25, 43] \; \wedge \; toy = ball$
THEN $sex = male$

Notice that two random values are selected for the numerical conditions though the entire range of values could also be valid, e.g., the condition 'toy's price IN [10, 50]'. Anyhow, this is not a problem since any individual having the antecedent or consequent with a maximum support produces a misleading rule, i.e., a lift value equal to unity, as explained in Section 2.1.

3.2. Evaluation Process

In this proposal, each individual I is evaluated according to two bounded range functions. The function F_{pool} uses a specific criterion to determine which in-

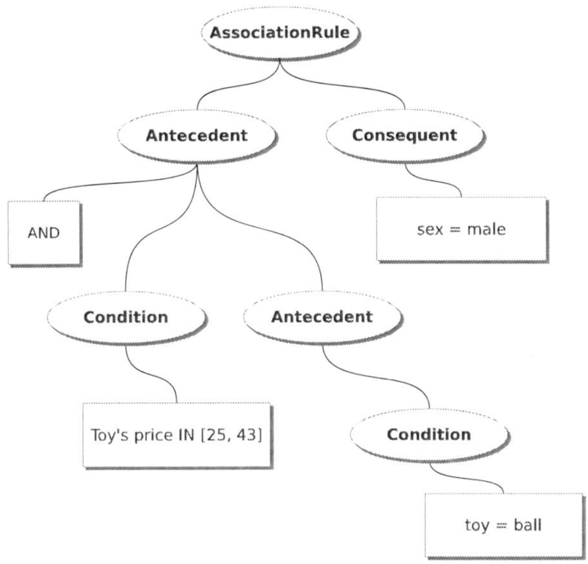

Figure 2. Sample derivation syntax-tree conformant to the grammar in Figure 1.

dividuals represent the best ARs. The other function, F, follows a different criterion to select indivuals whose structure is interesting for subsequent generations.

Notice that in the process of searching for the best rules, it is necessary to maximize the support, confidence, and lift. However, as shown in Equation 5, the confidence measure is maximized with the support measure, so we only need to maximize support and lift. Therefore, we propose a fitness function F_{pool} (see Equation 9) that maximizes support and lift and, in consequence, the three measures at once. F_{pool} is defined within the domain $[0, 1]$ and serves to determine the quality of the individuals in order to keep the best ones.

$$F_{pool}(I) = \begin{cases} sup(I) * lift(I) & \text{if } lift(I) > 1 \\ 0 & \text{otherwise} \end{cases} \quad (9)$$

On the other hand, it is essential to maintain the most promising rules in subsequent generations, so a different criterion is used for this. Firstly, it is interesting to obtain reliable rules, so those with high confidence values are desired. Secondly, it should be noted that very reliable rules could have low support values. Therefore, a function F to obtain reliable rules that do not appear infrequently is required (Equation 10), allowing of evolving individuals during the mining process. The range of values of this new function is $[0, 1]$.

$$F(I) = Conf(I) * F_{pool}(I) \tag{10}$$

3.3. Genetic Operators

In this proposal, a new parent selector based on a niche-crowding method has been constructed. Moreover, two genetic operators that follow a new interesting methodology in ARM are detailed in depth.

3.3.1. Parents Selector

The responsibility for obtaining a subset of individuals that act as parents in a given generation of the evolutionary process belongs to the selection operator, which is carried out in this proposal by implementing a niche-crowding [9, 10] model. This new model behaves like a clustering algorithm [20, 26], where individuals that satisfy similar instances belong to the same cluster. Thus, to determine the niche that each individual belongs to, the distance between two individuals (see Equation 11) is measured by comparing their instances covered, R_1 and R_2 being vectors having the instances covered by two rules, respectively.

$$distance(R_1, R_2) = 1 - \frac{R_1 \ R_2}{||R_1|| \ ||R_2||} \tag{11}$$

For a better understanding, consider the sample dataset shown in Table 1 and the instances covered by two sample rules, as depicted in Figure 3.

Instance in the dataset:	1 2 3 4 5 6 7 8 9 10
R_1) Bread → Milk:	1 0 0 0 0 1 0 0 0 0
R_2) Milk → Coffee:	1 0 0 0 0 1 0 0 1 0

Figure 3. Sample association rules.

In such a situation, the value of $R_1 \ R_2$ is 2, whereas the values of $||R_1||$ and $||R_2||$ are $\sqrt{2}$ and $\sqrt{3}$, respectively. Once these values are obtained, the distance between these two individuals is defined by $distance(R_1, R_2) = 1 - (2/(\sqrt{2}\sqrt{3})) = 0.194$. In consequence, since the range of the values is $[0, 1]$, both individuals tend to be closer. In such a way, the closer are two individuals, the more similar these individuals are.

In an iterative way, this parent selector aims to form niches comprising those individuals that cover similar instances. In an initial step, a number of individuals are selected to act as centroids for each niche. Then, each of the remaining individuals is assigned to the niche whose centroid is closer. Once every individual is assigned to a specific niche, the sum of distances of every individual to its centroid within a niche is obtained ($Dist$). The goal is to minimize $Dist$.

For each iteration, the first step consists in choosing new centroids that allow of obtaining the best results. The individual with the highest distance to its centroid is used as a new centroid, replacing the closer centroid. The process is carried out in an iterative way until $Dist$ can not be improved any more.

Once the iterations are finished, the parent selector operator randomly selects individuals from random niches each time. Thus, the aim is to cross individuals from different niches, which represent dissimilar rules.

3.3.2. Crossover Operator

The crossover procedure requires a set of individuals to act as parents, returning a set of new individuals. During this procedure, this genetic operator gets iteratively two individuals and then, according to an initial crossover probability, a random value will determine if the operation will be executed or not. In G3PARM+, the crossover probability is updated in each generation. If the average lift obtained in the pool of individuals is greater than that calculated in the previous generation, then the crossover probability will be increased since a depth search or exploitation is required. On the other hand, if the average lift is less than or equal to that obtained in the previous generation, then the crossover probability should be decreased.

This operator obtains new individuals from parents previously selected by the parent selector. In this paper, the crossover operator acts by swapping the most promising condition from each individual, i.e., the condition that allows further improvement of the support of the entire rule. Thereby, two offsprings are obtained having the most promising conditions swapped. If two conditions are equally promising, the one with the lowest absolute support will be selected. Additionally, if two conditions have the same absolute support, then one of them will be randomly selected.

For a better understanding, assume the rule $(Bread \wedge Milk) \rightarrow Coffee$

Instances in the dataset:	1 2 3 4 5 6 7 8 9 10
Bread:	1 0 1 1 0 1 0 1 0 0
Milk:	1 1 0 0 1 1 1 0 1 0
Coffee:	1 0 0 0 0 1 0 0 1 1
(Bread ∧ Milk) → Coffee:	1 0 0 0 0 1 0 0 0 0

(a) Instances covered by a sample rule

Instances in the dataset:	1 2 3 4 5 6 7 8 9 10
Bread:	1 0 1 1 0 1 0 1 **0** 0
Milk:	1 1 0 0 1 1 1 0 1 0
Coffee:	1 0 0 0 0 1 0 0 1 1
Bread:	0 0 0 0 0 0 0 0 **1** 0

(b) Condition *Bread* could improve the rule at most in one instance

Instances in the dataset:	1 2 3 4 5 6 7 8 9 10
Bread:	1 0 1 1 0 1 0 1 0 0
Milk:	1 1 0 0 1 1 1 0 1 0
Coffee:	1 0 0 0 0 1 0 0 1 1
Milk:	0 0 0 0 0 0 0 0 0 0

(c) Condition *Milk* could not improve the rule

Instances in the dataset:	1 2 3 4 5 6 7 8 9 10
Bread:	1 0 1 1 0 1 0 1 0 0
Milk:	1 1 0 0 1 1 1 0 1 0
Coffee:	1 0 0 0 0 1 0 0 1 1
Coffee:	0 0 0 0 0 0 0 0 0 0

(d) Condition *Coffee* could not improve the rule

Figure 4. Instances covered by each condition.

illustrated in Figure 4(a), which is based on the sample dataset depicted in Table 1. Once each condition is analysed, if the condition *Bread* is changed (see Figure 4(b)), it would possible to obtain a new condition that allows of covering one more instance. On the other hand, no instance might be affected if *Milk* (see Figure 4(c)) or *Coffee* (see Figure 4(d)) are selected. Replacing one of these two conditions, the maximum support that it would possible to obtain is the same that the support obtained using the original conditions. Therefore, the most promising condition to be changed is *Bread* since an absolute support of three could be obtained.

G3PARM addresses the issue of obtaning new individuals by changing the condition with the lowest support value within a rule. Sometimes, this methodology is not the best choice, as depicted in Figure 4. If the condition with the lowest support of the sample rule is changed, i.e., the condition *Coffee*, which has a support value of 0.4, then the entire rule could not be improved. Changing this condition, the support of the rule remains the same or even lower. However, using the crossover operator presented in this paper, the best condition to be replaced is *Bread*, which is not the lowest support condition, but the most promising condition. If this condition is altered, the support of the rule could be improved in one instance, so a support value of 0.3 could be obtained at most.

3.3.3. Mutation Operator

The mutation genetic operator is responsible for obtaining a new individual from another one previously selected. This operator also requires an initial mutation probability, which is responsible for determining whether certain individual will be mutated. This genetic operator modifies the most promising condition from a parent to obtain a better one. Similarly to the crossover probability, the mutation probability is updated in each generation as follows. If the average lift obtained in the pool of individuals is greater than that calculated in the previous generation, then the mutation probability decreases. On the other hand, if the average lift value is less than or equal to that obtained in the previous generation, then the mutation probability increases since a breadth search is required.

Additionally, a procedure to improve the reliability of the rules is also implemented in this operator. As mentioned in Section 2.1, the confidence of an associaton rule is maximum iff the set of instances covered by the antecedent of a rule is a subset of that covered by the consequent. Bearing in mind this, and considering that the support and the lift measures are symmetrical, then the procedure here implemented swaps the antecedent and consequent of a rule if its consequent support value is lower than its antecedent support value. In such a way, both the support and the lift remain the same, while the confidence will improve.

3.4. Update Process

G3PARM+ keeps the best individuals in a pool, i.e., those with a high quality, maintaining a good spread of solutions. An updating of this pool is required in each generation, adding those new individuals that exceed a quality level and removing the worst ones. This quality level is measured using the fitness F_{pool}, as described in Section 3.2. Individuals are ranked in a list and then, the pool is filled with the best ones using an iteratively procedure. This procedure avoids to keep individuals that cover the same instances, so no equivalent individuals are mined.

The pseudocode of the complete updating process is shown in Listing 1. In this procedure, the set $auxSet$ is initialized to the set $currentPopulation$, which comprises the individuals of the current population. Then, this set is filled with those new individuals within the sets $newPopulation$ and $pool$ (line 1). While the former is obtained using the crossover and mutation operators, the latter represents the pool of individuals belonging to the last generation. It should be noted that no repeated individual is added to the set $auxSet$. Finally, this set is ranked according to the function F_{pool} (line 2).

Once the set of individuals is obtained and ranked, the update of the new pool of individuals is carried out (lines 5 to 33). At the beginning, the best individual from the ranked set $auxSet$ is added to the pool $newPool$, which serves as the starting individual when the pool is empty. Then, for every individual $individualAux$ in the set $auxSet$, the algorithm checks whether there exists any rule in the set $newPool$ that already covers the same instances (line 10). If there is such an individual and, furthermore, their lift values are equal, then the one with the higher confidence value is kept in this pool (lines 11 to 15). However, if both have the same confidence value, the one with the lowest number of conditions is added for comprensibility purposes (lines 17 to 20). In this way, the proposal searches for small rules with a high confidence. Finally, the set of individuals $newPool$ is returned.

It should be noted that, since G3PARM+ updates the pool of individuals by analysing the instances covered by each new rule, the resulting set of rules will be very representative of the domain under study and, therefore, the resulting set obtains a high coverage value.

Listing 1 Update process

Input: *pool*, *currentPopulation*, *newPopulation*, *poolSize*
Output: *newPool*

```
auxSet ← auxSet ∪ obtainNotRepeatedIndividuals(currentPopulation,
    newPopulation, pool)
auxSet ← rankIndividuals(auxSet,F_pool)
i ← 0
newPool ← ∅
for all individualAux ∈ auxSet do
    if getSize(newPool) = 0 then
        newPool ← individualAux
    else
        for all individualPool ∈ newPool do
            if instancesCovered(individualAux) = instancesCovered(individualPool)
            then
                if calculateLift(individualAux) = calculateLift(individualPool) then
                    if calculateConfidence(individualAux) >
                    calculateConfidence(individualPool) then
                        newPool ← newPool\{individualPool}
                        newPool ← newPool ∪ individualAux
                        break
                    else
                        if calculateConfidence(individualAux) =
                        calculateConfidence(individualPool) AND
                        calculateConditions(individualAux) <
                        calculateConditions(individualPool) then
                            newPool ← newPool\{individualPool}
                            newPool ← newPool ∪ individualAux
                            break
                        end if
                    end if
                end if
            else
                newPool ← newPool ∪ individualAux
                break
            end if
        end for
    end if
    if getSize(newPool) = poolSize then
        break
    end if
end for
return newPool
```

3.5. The ARM Algorithm

The algorithm proposed (see Figure 5 for a general sketch) uses two populations with a prefixed size: one to maintain the most promising individuals obtained throughout the generations, and the other to keep those individuals that should not be lost because of their high-quality. The algorithm starts by randomly generating individuals conformant to the CFG defined in Figure 1. Those individuals that cover at least one instance are added to the population, so it comprises only rules with a support greater than zero. It is an iteratively process, adding individuals until the pool size is reached. On the other hand, and in order to obtain new individuals in each generation, a set of parents is chosen from the current population and the pool of individuals. Since the pool of individuals is empty in the first generation, parents are chosen only from the current population. The parent selector procedure allows of selecting individuals from different niches, as explained in Section 3.3.1, providing a set of individuals from the application of the mutation and crossover operators, as described in Section 3.3.2 and 3.3.3.

After applying these operators, a new set of individuals is obtained and added to a new population, also comprising the current population and the pool of individuals. It is worth mentioning that this approach avoids the repetition of individuals in this new population. At this point, the algorithm is divided into two paths, none being dependent on the other. The easiest path is responsible for updating the next population of the evolutionary process. With this purpose, the algorithm ranks the individuals within the new population previously obtained. This ranking procedure is carried out by using the F function described in Section 3.2, so the best individuals are selected to be part of the new population. On the contrary, the second path is responsible for updating the pool of individuals by running the procedure described in Listing 1. In this case, the procedure ranks the individuals according to the F_{pool} function, being selected the best ones as described in Section 3.4. Once this procedure is completed, the pool of individuals is checked. If the average lift of this set of individuals is greater than that calculated in the previous generation, it means that the population is improving, so a lower diversity is required. In such a situation, the crossover probability increases and the mutation probability decreases. On the other hand, if the average lift is less than or equal to that obtained in the previous generation, a higher diversity is necessary, so the crossover probability decreases and the mutation probability increases.

Unlike other existing evolutionary ARM algorithms, an important feature of

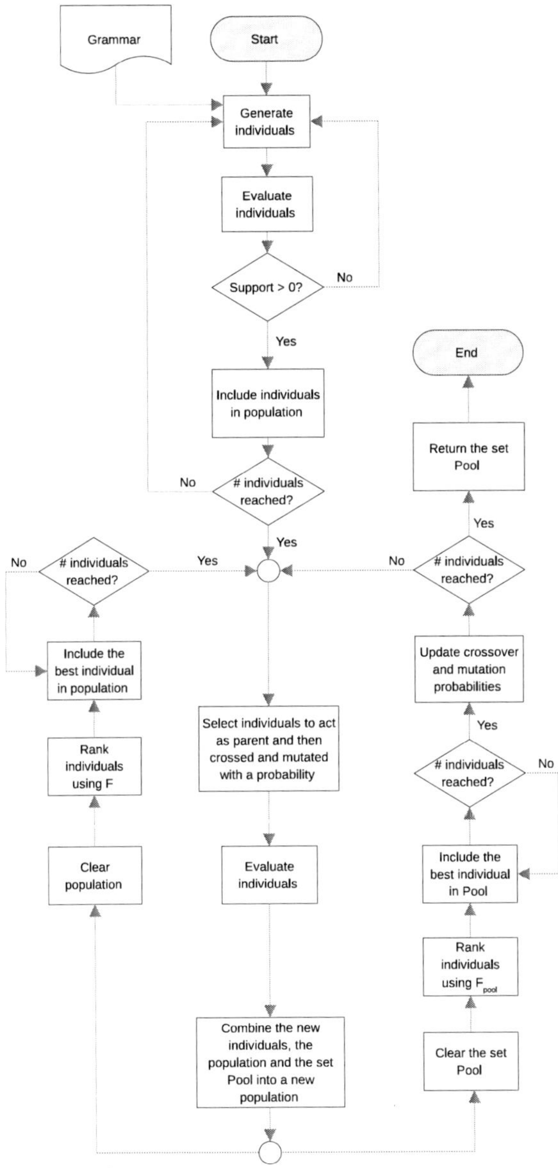

Figure 5. The flowchart for the proposed algorithm.

this algorithm is that the number of parameters required is low. Specifically, the continuous updating of the crossover and mutation probabilities mitigates the difficulty of using this algorithm by non-expert users. Additionally, G3PARM+ does not require establishing minimum thresholds, so it does not require a previous knowledge of the domain under application.

4. Experimental Study

In this paper, several experiments were carried out, using a variety of 17 datasets[1] with different numbers of instances and attributes (see Table 3), to demonstrate the effectiveness of the proposal presented. G3PARM was originally compared with other exhaustive search (Apriori and FP-Growth) and evolutionary algorithms (ARMGA and QuantMiner) in [21], providing great results. At a significance level of $p = 0.05$, G3PARM was significantly different from exhaustive search algorithms in support and confidence measures. Focus-

Table 3. Datasets

Dataset	Abbreviation	#Instances	#Attributes	Type
Automobile	*Autom*	392	8	Num.
Ankara Weather	*Ankara*	1608	10	Num.
Chess	*Chess*	3196	37	Categ.
Connect-4	*Con4*	7557	43	Categ.
Credit German	*Credit*	1000	21	Categ., Num.
House_16H	*HH*	22784	17	Num.
Izmir Weather	*Izmir*	1461	10	Num.
Low Birth Weight	*LBW*	189	10	Categ., Num.
Mushroom	*Mush*	8124	23	Categ.
Nursery	*Nurs*	12960	9	Categ.
Primary Tumor	*Prim*	339	18	Categ.
Soybean	*Soyb*	683	36	Categ.
Splice	*Splice*	3190	61	Categ.
Treasury	*Treas*	1049	16	Categ.
Wisc. Diagn. Cancer	*WDBC*	569	31	Categ., Num.
Wisc. Progn. Cancer	*WPBC*	194	34	Categ., Num.
Zoo	*Zoo*	102	17	Categ.

[1] All these datasets are publicly available for download from the UCI machine learning repository (http://archive.ics.uci.edu/ml/datasets).

ing on evolutionary algorithms and the support measure, at a significance level of $p = 0.05$, G3PARM was significantly different from the other algorithms. On the other hand, studying the confidence measure, G3PARM was significantly different from QuantMiner, but not from ARMGA. Thus, a comparison of the new proposal versus G3PARM is made in this experimental stage.

All the experiments carried out in this study were performed on an Intel Core i7 machine with 12GB main memory and running CentOS 5.4. Moreover, G3PARM and the proposal presented in this paper were written by using JCLEC [2] [32], a Java library for evolutionary computation.

In the following subsections, first the experimental set-up is presented. Then, a study of the adaptiveness of the crossover and mutation probabilities is examined, and the results obtained are discussed. Next, an analysis of the influence of varying the number of generations is presented. Finally, a series of experiments serve to contrast the scalability of the algorithms as well as how they behave on increasing the number of attributes and the number of instances in the dataset.

4.1. Experimental Set-up

The evolutionary proposal here presented only requires four parameters to be determined by the expert: the population size, the maximum number of generations, the maximum derivation size, and the pool size. To achieve a fair comparison with the G3PARM algorithm, their values remain the same as those provided in [21]. These optimal parameters are shown in Table 4, where the best results for G3PARM were obtained using a population size of 50 individuals, 100 generations, 70% crossover probability, 14% mutation probability, and a maximum derivation size of 24.

The results shown for each algorithm in the following experimental study are the average values calculated running each one 30 times with different seeds.

4.2. Crossover and Mutation Probabilities

A major feature of G3PARM+ is its ability to update both genetic operator probabilities. To show this, Figure 6 lists the crossover and mutation probability values in each generation for a sample execution. Notice that in the first generation both measures have the initial value 0.5.

[2]JCLEC is publicly available for download from http://jclec.sf.net

Table 4. Optimal parameters

Parameter	G3PARM+	G3PARM
Population size	50	50
Pool	20	20
Number of generations	100	100
Maximum derivation size	24	24
Crossover probability	-	70%
Mutation probability	-	14%
Confidence threshold	-	90%
Support threshold	-	70%

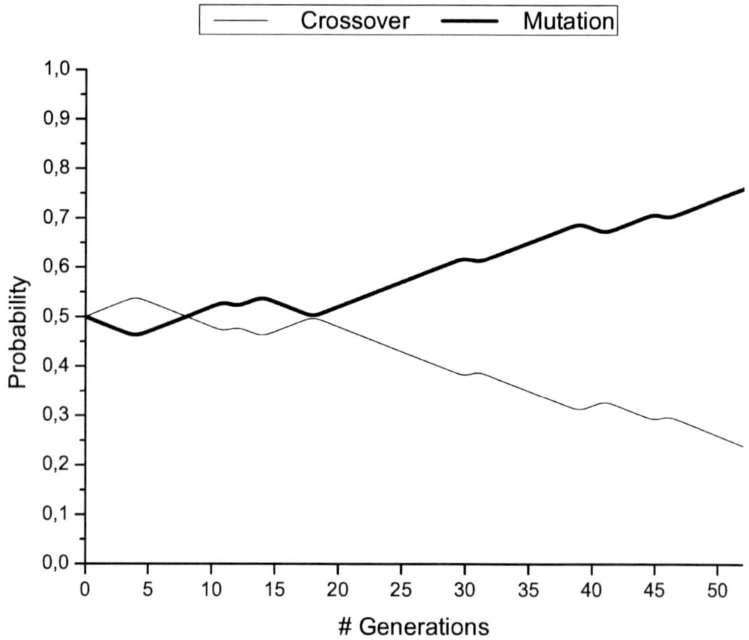

Figure 6. Crossover and mutation probabilities along the generations.

In subsequent generations, these probabilities are updated. It is interesting to note that in the earliest generations, both probabilities increase and decrease while the optimal average lift value is not found. Then, the mutation probability begins to increase whereas the crossover probability decreases. This means that the average lift is not improving and, therefore, the optimal value is obtained.

Table 5. Average results obtained for mushroom and nursery datasets

	Mushroom dataset			Nursery dataset	
Measures	G3PARM+	G3PARM	Measures	G3PARM+	G3PARM
Support	0.991	1.000	**Support**	0.663	0.759
Confidence	0.999	1.000	**Confidence**	0.971	0.990
Lift	1.005	1.000	**Lift**	1.105	1.003
#Rules	20.000	20.000	**#Rules**	20.000	2.967

Nevertheless, despite the average lift value not being improved, it is possible to obtain other different and interesting rules, so the evolutionary process must go on, at least for a certain number of generations.

4.3. Analysis of the Results

As discussed in Section 2.1, the use of a support–confidence framework could cause unexpected values in some domains, so new measures are required to mine interesting rules. To clarify this assertion, the mushroom and nursery datasets were used and the average results obtained are shown in Table 5. Using the mushroom dataset, G3PARM mined a set of 20 rules and every rule had a maximal support value. As expected, its confidence value is maximal too. Furthermore, maximal support values provide misleading rules, so their lift values are equal to unity. This clarifies that the goal of ARM is not only the extraction of frequent and reliable rules, but interesting rules are required too.

On the other hand, attending to the nursery dataset, the average number of rules mined by executing the G3PARM algorithm 30 times is 2.967. Every execution was performed while setting the thresholds to 70% and 90% for the support and confidence measures, respectively. Moreover, the size of the population to be returned was set to 20. As mentioned above, the use of these thresholds requires an exhaustive knowledge of the dataset used, and the results obtained for the nursery dataset is a clear example.

Globally, the average results of the experiments performed over different datasets are shown in Table 6, where the best results for each measure are written in bold typeface. Notice that the two datasets mentioned above were not considered, due to their problems. Studying the support measure values, which are shown in Table 6(a), it is worth mentioning that the new proposal mines more frequent rules than G3PARM, obtaining an average difference value of 0.023.

Table 6. Average results obtained for different datasets

(a) Average support values obtained with different datasets

Dataset	G3PARM+	G3PARM
Ankara	**0.987**	0.940
Autom	**0.958**	0.862
Chess	**0.947**	0.898
Con4	**0.992**	0.946
Credit	**0.966**	0.925
HH	**0.999**	0.958
Izmir	**0.989**	0.958
LBW	0.929	**0.944**
Prim	**0.917**	0.836
Soyb	0.901	**0.925**
Splice	0.984	**0.999**
Treas	**0.944**	0.894
WDBC	**0.991**	0.982
WPBC	**0.980**	0.952
Zoo	0.667	**0.780**

(b) Average confidence values obtained with different datasets

Dataset	G3PARM+	G3PARM
Ankara	0.995	**0.999**
Autom	**0.988**	**0.988**
Chess	0.993	**1.000**
Con4	0.998	**1.000**
Credit	0.987	**0.999**
HH	**1.000**	**1.000**
Izmir	0.996	**0.999**
LBW	0.981	**0.997**
Prim	0.976	**0.994**
Soyb	0.995	**0.999**
Splice	**1.000**	**1.000**
Treas	0.990	**1.000**
WDBC	0.997	**1.000**
WPBC	0.995	**1.000**
Zoo	**0.976**	0.973

(c) Average lift values obtained with different datasets

Dataset	G3PARM+	G3PARM
Ankara	1.001	**1.004**
Autom	1.011	**1.024**
Chess	**1.148**	1.004
Con4	1.001	**1.002**
Credit	**1.001**	1.000
HH	**1.001**	1.000
Izmir	**1.001**	**1.001**
LBW	**1.019**	1.002
Prim	**1.006**	1.003
Soyb	**1.134**	1.013
Splice	**22.260**	1.000
Treas	1.045	**1.049**
WDBC	**1.002**	**1.002**
WPBC	**1.007**	**1.007**
Zoo	**1.490**	1.055

(d) Average coverage values obtained with different datasets

Dataset	G3PARM+	G3PARM
Ankara	**1.000**	**1.000**
Autom	**1.000**	0.989
Chess	**1.000**	0.999
Con4	**1.000**	**1.000**
Credit	**1.000**	**1.000**
HH	**1.000**	**1.000**
Izmir	**1.000**	**1.000**
LBW	0.998	**1.000**
Prim	0.999	**1.000**
Soyb	**1.000**	0.999
Splice	**1.000**	**1.000**
Treas	**0.993**	0.961
WDBC	**1.000**	0.999
WPBC	0.998	**1.000**
Zoo	**1.000**	0.995

Focusing on the confidence measure (see Table 6(b)), the results show that using G3PARM, the average confidence values obtained for each dataset are greater than those acquired using the new proposal. Although G3PARM+ does not provide the best confidence values, the average difference between both algorithms is very low, just a value of 0.005, discovering very reliable rules too.

Studying the results presented in Table 6(c), G3PARM+ discovers very interesting rules in most datasets, since their values are greater than unity. Some remarkable results are those that obtain a low lift value, close to unity. However, it should be noted that these results are interesting since it obtains rules which are frequent, reliable, and interesting all at once. Calculating the average difference between the lift values obtained by both algorithms, a value of 1.464 is obtained.

Finally, Table 6(d) shows the average coverage measure for each dataset and algorithm. This measure represents the percentage (in a per unit basis) of instances covered by the resulting set of rules. Focusing on this measure, note that while the new proposal wins in 12 out of 15 datasets, the G3PARM algorithm wins in 9 out of 15 datasets. The average results of all the datasets demonstrate that using this measure, G3PARM+ obtains better results than G3PARM, calculating a difference value of 0.003.

Table 7 shows the average number of attributes per rule for the resulting set and the average amplitude of the numerical attributes for this set, respectively.

Table 7. Average number of attributes and amplitude obtained for different datasets

(a) Average number of attributes

Dataset	G3PARM	G3PARM+
Ankara	**2.82**	2.91
Autom	2.78	**2.49**
Chess	**2.99**	3.01
Con4	3.63	**3.05**
Credit	**2.59**	2.81
HH	**2.80**	3.16
Izmir	**2.81**	3.14
LBW	**2.60**	3.01
Prim	2.75	**2.26**
Soyb	3.05	**2.65**
Splice	3.14	**2.42**
Treas	2.83	**2.72**
WDBC	2.95	**2.80**
WPBC	**2.87**	2.88
Zoo	**3.07**	3.11

(b) Average amplitude (in percentage)

Dataset	G3PARM+	G3PARM
Ankara	81.56	**76.06**
Autom	84.98	**75.26**
Chess	-	-
Con4	-	-
Credit	**77.95**	78.15
HH	81.48	**70.73**
Izmir	89.71	**73.19**
LBW	**79.15**	79.83
Prim	-	-
Soyb	-	-
Splice	-	-
Treas	-	-
WDBC	79.11	**59.27**
WPBC	84.55	**75.26**
Zoo	-	-

Table 8. Wilcoxon signed rank test results obtained for different measures

Measure	p-value	W+	W-
Support	0.041	96	24
Confidence	0.002	3	75
Lift	0.151	57.5	20.5
Coverage	0.301	31.5	13.5
#Attributes	0.248	72	48
Amplitude	0.018	3	33

For the second value, only numerical datasets have been considered. Notice that there is no difference in the average number of attributes for both algorithms. This number of attributes is not constrained a priori. As for the amplitude, G3PARM divides the range of values into a number of equal-width points and uses these cut-points as values for the numerical attributes. On the contrary, G3PARM+ does not require any number of equal-width cut-points, so ranges of any amplitude could be obtained. For example, using 5 equal-width cut-points, G3PARM could obtain an amplitude of value 80% at most, whereas G3PARM+ is not restricted in this sense.

Although this analysis is based on the average values of several measures over datasets that have different features, a more accurate statistical analysis is required. With this purpose, the Wilcoxon signed rank test [8] (see Table 8 where the sum of all positive ranks (W+) and all negative ranks (W-) are depicted) has been performed, obtaining a p-value of 0.041 for the support measure, so it is possible to assert that there are significant differences between G3PARM and G3PARM+ using a significance level of $\alpha = 0.05$, the latter being statistically better. Obtaining the sum of all ranks, it is stated that the sum of all positive ranks is 96, whereas the sum of all negative ranks is 24. Continuing with the analysis, a p-value of 0.002 is calculated for the confidence measure. Here, the sum of all positive ranks is 3, whereas the sum of all negative ranks is 75. Using a significance level of $\alpha = 0.05$, we can state that G3PARM is statistically better for the confidence measure with significant differences.

Focusing on the lift measure, the test reveals a p-value of 0.151 for the lift measure, the sum of all positive and negative ranks being 57.5 and 20.5, respectively. Consequently, it is not possible to assert that there are significant differences between both approaches, though G3PARM+ seems to behave better. Additionally, it is not possible to assert that there are significant differences between both algorithms using the coverage measure, obtaining a p-value of

0.301. Under these circumstances, it is necessary to determine which one is statistically better, so the sum of all positive and negative ranks are calculated. The results show that the positive ranks sum to 31.5 whereas the negative ranks sum to 13.5. In consequence, it is possible to assert that, despite the fact that there are no significant differences between the proposals, G3PARM+ is statistically better. As for the number of attributes obtained, this test reveals a p-value of 0.248, so it is not possible to assert that there are significant differences between both algorithms, even when G3PARM+ behaves better considering that the sum of all positive ranks is 72. Finally, regarding the amplitude of the numerical intervals, a p-value of 0.018 is obtained, stating that there are significant differences when a significance level of $\alpha = 0.05$ is calculated, G3PARM being statistically better.

This statistical analysis shows that G3PARM+ behaves better in four out of six measures, obtaining differences in support value for a significance level of $\alpha = 0.05$. As for the Lift and coverage measures, G3PARM+ behaves better than G3PARM. Finally, G3PARM obtains the best confidence values. Noted that, unlike G3PARM+, G3PARM mines rules with only one attribute in the consequent, limiting the type of rules which can be discovered. Since the consequent is composed of only one condition, the support of the consequent can be higher easily and, therefore, the confidence values are likely to be higher. Finally, it is interesting to point out that the number of attributes obtained by G3PARM+ is slightly lower than by G3PARM, as expected after the analysis of the support values obtained. Notice that the higher is the support value of a rule, the lower is its number of attributes.

4.4. Influence of the Number of Generations

In order to observe the effect of varying the number of generations on the proposed algorithm, a number of experiments were carried out over the *Primary Tumor* dataset. Here, the behaviour of G3PARM and G3PARM+ are described for support, confidence, lift and coverage measures (see Figure 7).

Focusing on the support measure, whereas G3PARM+ increases its values when the number of generations grows, G3PARM comes to a standstill in early generations, as shown in Figure 7(a). In such a situation, the support can not be improved anymore, so the average confidence grows, as depicted in Figure 7(b). On the other hand, G3PARM+ allows of increasing the average support in every generation. Focusing on the average confidence value, the new model allows

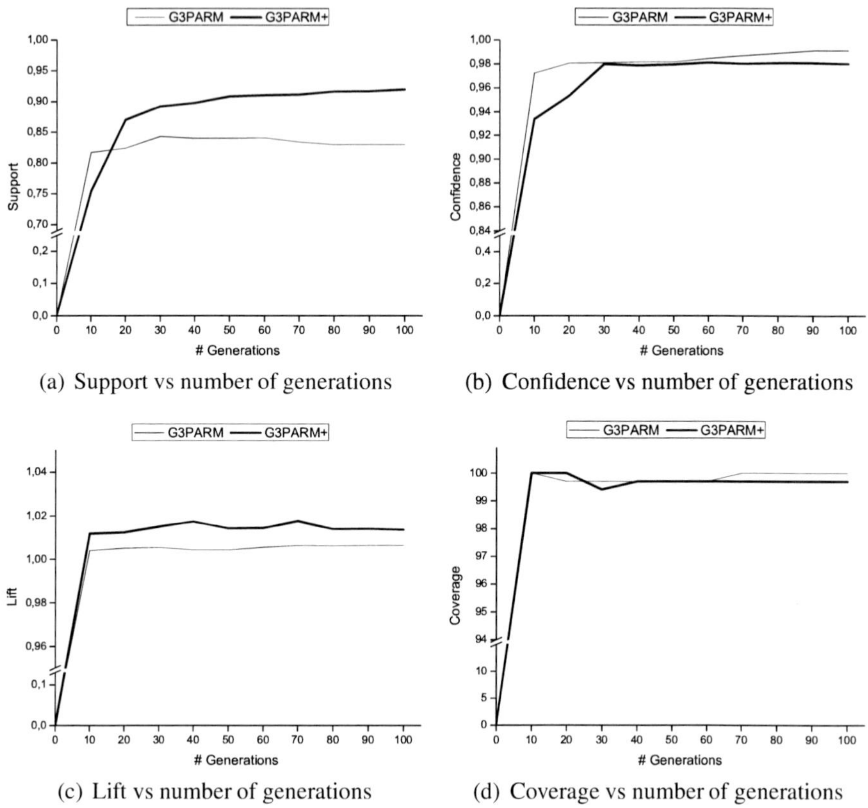

(a) Support vs number of generations

(b) Confidence vs number of generations

(c) Lift vs number of generations

(d) Coverage vs number of generations

Figure 7. Influence of the variation of the number of generations in different measures.

of obtaining almost the same average values as those obtained with G3PARM. Therefore, a global analysis of the average support and confidence measures reveals that the behaviour of the new model is better.

Figure 7(c) shows the average lift values obtained in different generations. Whereas G3PARM+ obtains the best average lift values, G3PARM discovers rules whose lift values are close to unity. Finally, analysing the coverage measure (see Figure 7(d)), both G3PARM and the new algorithm obtained values close to 100% in terms of the percentage of instances covered by the resulting set.

4.5. Analysis of the Scalability

Since G3PARM+ uses two different functions to evaluate each measure and a specific analysis to group the individuals in niches, it is possible to think that the computation time has increased significantly in comparison to G3PARM. However, this situation does not occurr as shown by the following analysis.

A number of experiments were also carried out to analyse the computation time of G3PARM and G3PARM+ over two different datasets, as depicted in Figure 8. The Y-axis represents the time in milliseconds, whereas the X-axis stands for the percentage of instances (% Instances) using all attributes or the

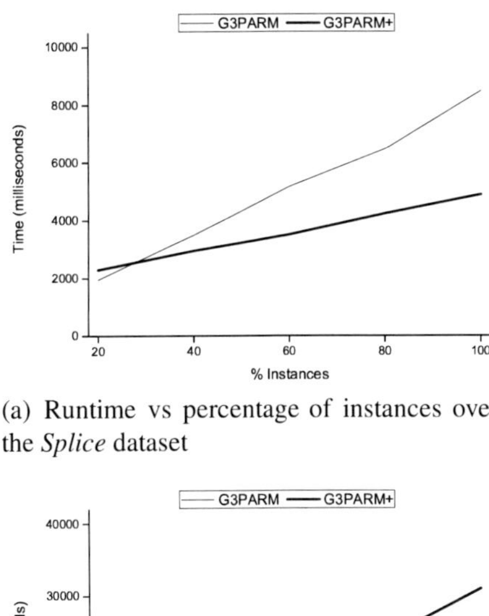

(a) Runtime vs percentage of instances over the *Splice* dataset

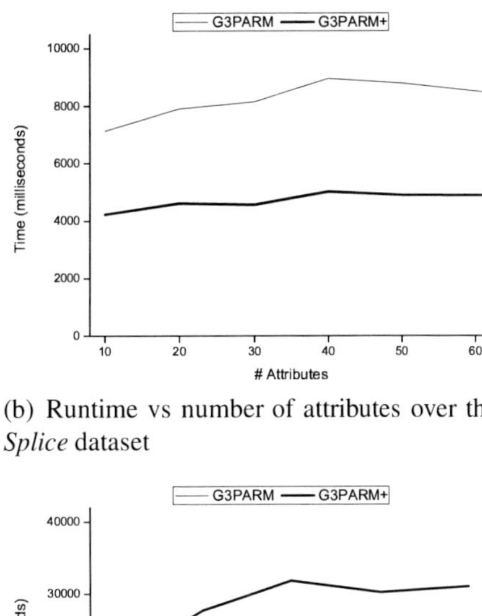

(b) Runtime vs number of attributes over the *Splice* dataset

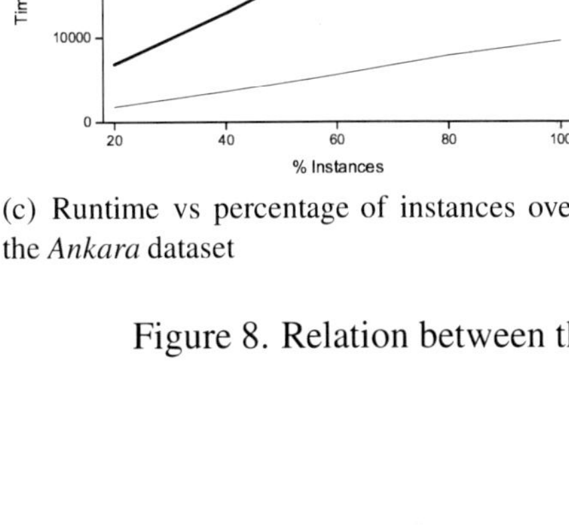

(c) Runtime vs percentage of instances over the *Ankara* dataset

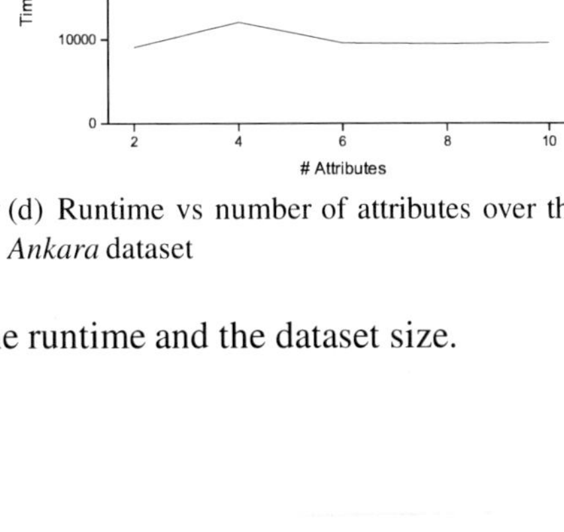

(d) Runtime vs number of attributes over the *Ankara* dataset

Figure 8. Relation between the runtime and the dataset size.

number of attributes (# Attributes) using all the instances.

Figures 8(a) and 8(b) show the runtimes for the *Splice* dataset, all its attributes being categorical. Focusing on Figure 8(a), it should be noted that G3PARM+ scales better than G3PARM, which seems to increase exponentially. On the other hand, analysing the results plotted in Figure 8(b), note that both algorithms behave similarly, G3PARM+ expending a lower computational time in this case. However, studying the behaviour of a different dataset, i.e., *Ankara*, which defines all of its attributes in a numerical domain, it is seen that G3PARM+ scales worse than G3PARM, as shown in Figures 8(c) and 8(d).

Apparently, G3PARM+ scales better over categorical than over numerical attributes, as expected. Nevertheless, the use of the operators IN and OUT requires a more complex evaluation since they require analysing whether a value is within a range or not. On the other hand, note that in G3PARM these operators are not defined and the evaluation process only requires checking whether a value is less than or greater than the other. An important advantage of the operators IN and OUT is their interpretability by the data miner, giving intervals that are difficult to be obtained using traditional numerical operators.

5. Concluding Remarks

In this paper, a novel G3P algorithm for mining ARs was presented. Recently, a promising G3P algorithm, called G3PARM, was proposed for mining frequent and reliable rules. That algorithm was compared to existing proposals in the ARM field, both exhaustive search and evolutionary algorithms, obtaining interesting results. G3PARM has a number of parameters that should be established before its execution, which may require previous knowledge. This makes quite difficult its use by non-experts. The algorithm proposed in this paper, called G3PARM+, is a self-adaptive proposal, which does not require as many configuration parameters as other previous proposals do (e.g., any threshold for support and confidence). Another strong point is that no previous knowledge about the dataset is needed.

One of the main drawbacks of the support–confidence framework is the discovery of misleading rules, as discussed in Section 2.1. To avoid this weakness, G3PARM+ proposes the use of the lift measure as well, which indicates how interesting a rule is. Since this measure is not bounded above, two fitness functions were conceived, lift being weighted by the support measure, obtaining values within the range [0,1].

This new algorithm allows the discovery of rules with any number of conditions in both the antecedent and consequent. Moreover, the rules mined are constrained by a CFG, which provides expressiveness and flexibility, and permits of exploring both numerical and categorical domains. In order to mine new individuals in a given generation of the evolutionary process, it provides two genetic operators that work over the most promising conditions. Furthermore, for the sake of grouping similar rules, G3PARM+ implements a niche-crowding method that uses the scalar product to determine the distance between rules. Finally, the resulting set of rules returns dissimilar rules, this set being highly representative of the whole dataset as demonstrated by the coverage measure. Concluding, an experimental study was performed, demonstrating that G3PARM+ obtains interesting rules with high support and confidence values.

References

[1] R. Agrawal, T. Imielinski, and A. N. Swami. Mining Association Rules between Sets of Items in Large Databases. In *SIGMOD Conference, Proceedings of the 1993 ACM SIGMOD International Conference on Management of Data, Washington, DC*, pages 207–216, May 1993.

[2] R. Agrawal and R. Srikant. Fast Algorithms for Mining Association Rules in Large Databases. In J. B. Bocca, M. Jarke, and C. Zaniolo, editors, *VLDB'94, Proceedings of 20th International Conference on Very Large Data Bases, Santiago de Chile, Chile*, pages 487–499. Morgan Kaufmann, September 1994.

[3] K. I. Ahn and J. Y. Kim. Efficient Mining of Frequent Itemsets and a Measure of Interest for Association Rule Mining. *Journal of Information & Knowledge Management*, 3(3):245–257, 2004.

[4] B. Alatas and E. Akin. An Efficient Genetic Algorithm for Automated Mining of Both Positive and Negative Quantitative Association Rules. *Soft Computing*, 10:230–237, 2006.

[5] J. Alcala-Fdez, N. Flugy-Pape, A. Bonarini, and F. Herrera. Analysis of the Effectiveness of the Genetic Algorithms based on Extraction of Association Rules. *Fundamenta Informatica*, 98(1):1001–1014, 2010.

[6] C. Borgelt. Efficient Implementations of Apriori and Eclat. In *FIMI'03, 1st Workshop on Frequent Itemset Mining Implementations, Melbourne, FL, USA*, December 2003.

[7] S. Brin, R. Motwani, and C. Silverstein. Beyond market baskets: generalizing association rules to correlations. In *1997 ACM SIGMOD, Proceedings of 1997 International Conference on Management of Data*, pages 265–276, 1997.

[8] J. Demšar. Statistical Comparisons of Classifiers over Multiple Data Sets. *The Journal of Machine Learning Research*, 7:1–30, 2006.

[9] G. Dick and P. Whigham. Spatially-Structured Evolutionary Algorithms and Sharing: Do They Mix? In *Simulated Evolution and Learning*, volume 4247 of *Lecture Notes in Computer Science*, pages 457–464. Springer-Verlag, Berlin, 2006.

[10] G. Dick and P. Whigham. Spatially-Structured Sharing Technique for Multimodal Problems. *Journal of Computer Science and Technology*, 23:64–76, 2008.

[11] P. G. Espejo, S. Ventura, and F. Herrera. A Survey on the Application of Genetic Programming to Classification. *IEEE Transactions on Systems, Man and Cybernetics: Part C*, 40(2):121–144, 2010.

[12] F. Berzal and I. Blanco and D. Sánchez and M. A. Vila. Measuring the Accuracy and Interest of Association Rules: A new Framework. *Intelligent Data Analysis*, 6(3):221–235, 2002.

[13] A. A. Freitas. *Data Mining and Knowledge Discovery with Evolutionary Algorithms*. Springer-Verlag, Berlin, 2002.

[14] J. Han, J. Pei, Y. Yin, and R. Mao. Mining Frequent Patterns without Candidate Generation: A Frequent-Pattern Tree Approach. *Data Mining and Knowledge Discovery*, 8:53–87, 2004.

[15] I. Mahdavi and M. Movahednejad and F. Adbesh. Designing customer-oriented catalogs in e-CRM using an effective self-adaptive genetic algorithm. *Expert Systems with Applications*, 38(1):631–639, 2011.

[16] K. Taboada and K. Shimad and S. Mabu and K. Hirasawa and J. Hu. A self-adaptive migration model genetic algorithm for data mining applications. *Information Sciences*, 177(20):4295–4313, 2007.

[17] L. Ke-Chung, L. I-En, and C. Zhi-Sheng. An Improved Frequent Pattern Growth Method for Mining Association Rules. *Expert Systems With Applications*, 38:5154–5161, 2011.

[18] J. R. Koza. *Genetic Programming: On the Programming of Computers by Means of Natural Selection*. The MIT Press, December 1992.

[19] L. Geng and H. J. Hamilton. Interestingness Measures for Data Mining: A Survey. *ACM Computing Surveys*, 38, September 2006.

[20] J. Z. C. Laia and T. J. Huang. An agglomerative clustering algorithm using a dynamic k-nearest-neighbor list. *Information Sciences*, 181(9):1722–1734, 2011.

[21] J. M. Luna, J. R. Romero, and S. Ventura. Design and Behavior Study of a Grammar-guided Genetic Programming Algorithm for Mining Association Rules. *Knowledge and Information Systems*, 32(1):53–76, 2012.

[22] M. Martínez-Ballesteros, F. Martínez-Álvarez, A. Troncoso, and J. C. Riquelme. An evolutionary algorithm to discover quantitative association rules in multidimensional time series. *Soft Computing*, 15:2065–2084, 2011.

[23] M. Martínez-Ballesteros, S. Salcedo-Sanz, J. C. Riquelme, C. Casanova-Mateo, and J. L. Camacho. Evolutionary association rules for total ozone content modeling from satellite observations. *Chemometrics and Intelligent Laboratory Systems*, 109:217–227, 2011.

[24] J. Mata, J. L. Alvarez, and J. C. Riquelme. Discovering Numeric Association Rules via Evolutionary Algorithm. In *Advances in Knowledge Discovery and Data Mining*, volume 2336 of *Lecture Notes in Computer Science*, pages 40–51, 2002.

[25] R. McKay, N. Hoai, P. Whigham, Y. Shan, and M. ONeill. Grammar-based Genetic Programming: A Survey. *Genetic Programming and Evolvable Machines*, 11:365–396, 2010.

[26] W. D. Mulder. Optimal clustering in the context of overlapping cluster analysis. *Information Sciences*, 223(0):56–74, 2013.

[27] G. Piatetsky-Shapiro. Discovery, Analysis, and Presentation of Strong Rules. In *Knowledge Discovery in Databases*, pages 229–248. 1991.

[28] C. Romero, A. Zafra, J. Luna, and S. Ventura. Association rule mining using genetic programming to provide feedback to instructors from multiplechoice quiz data. *Expert Systems*, 30:162–172, 2013.

[29] A. Salleb-Aouissi, C. Vrain, and C. Nortet. QuantMiner: A Genetic Algorithm for Mining Quantitative Association Rules. In *IJCAI'97, Proceedings of the 20th International Joint Conference on Artificial Intelligence, Hyberadad, India*, pages 1035–1040, January 2007.

[30] Y. Shen, J. Liu, and Z. Yang. Research on Positive and Negative Association Rules based on Interest-Support-Confidence Framework. In *CiSE'09, Proceedings of the International Conference on Computational Intelligence and Software Engineering, Ravda, Bulgaria*, pages 1035–1040, June 2009.

[31] R. Srikant and R. Agrawal. Mining Quantitative Association Rules in Large Relational Tables. In *SIGMOD'96, Proceedings of the 1996 ACM SIGMOD International Conference on Management of Data, Montreal, Quebec, Canada*, pages 1–12, June 1996.

[32] S. Ventura, C. Romero, A. Zafra, J. A. Delgado, and C. Hervás. JCLEC: A Framework for Evolutionary Computation. *Soft Computing*, 12:381–392, 2007.

[33] X. Yan, C. Zhang, and S. Zhang. ARMGA: Identifying Interesting Association Rules with Genetic Algorithms. *Applied Artificial Intelligence*, 19(7):677–689, 2005.

[34] M. J. Zaki. Scalable Algorithms for Association Mining. *IEEE Transactions on Knowledge and Data Engineering*, 12(3):372–390, 2000.

[35] C. Zhang and S. Zhang. Association Rules Mining: Models and Algorithms. *Lecture Notes in Computer Science*, 2307:243, 2002.

INDEX

#

A

B

C

D

H

I

J

K

L

M

N

O

P

Q

R

S

T

U

V

W

X

Y

Z